INFINITE

IMPACT

THE ENTREPRENEUR'S STRATEGIC GUIDE
TO BOOKS & BUSINESS SUCCESS

AMBER VILHAUER

©2024 Amber Vilhauer
All rights reserved.

No part of this publication may be reproduced or transmitted in any form or by any means, electronic or mechanical, including photography, recording, or any information storage and retrieval system, without permission in writing from the author.

Requests for permission to make copies of any part of the work should be emailed to the following address:
amber@ngngenterprises.com.

Visit the author's website at ambervilhauer.com

Published and distributed by STRONGPrint Publishing
Colorado, USA

Library of Congress Number: 2024905583
Vilhauer, Amber

Infinite Impact:
The Entrepreneur's Strategic Guide to Books & Business Success

ISBN: 978-1-962074-19-3 Hardcover
ISBN: 978-1-962074-20-9 Paperback
ISBN: 978-1-962074-21-6 ebook

TO: YOU

It is time to get your cause out to the world in a much faster and more significant way. It is time to dig in and be the leader you know deep down you are meant to be. It is time to eliminate distractions, cultivate the right team to support you, and leverage your talent to scale your impact.

I invite you to embrace the qualities already inside you that mirror those of an eagle.

The eagle symbolizes staying grounded and looking forward with a careful eye to precisely design the future. When in flight, the eagle can soar to heights other birds merely dream of.

The scar on the shoulder of the NGNG (No Guts No Glory!) eagle represents the lessons from the past you had to learn the hard way—the lessons that made you stronger and ready to move forward with grace and determination.

When fear, doubt, or frustration creep in, remember your vision. Remember why you started your business. Remember all of the people out there who are ready to grow their life's meaning, being transformed by the cause you stand for.

Remember, No Guts No Glory!

xo,
AmberV

GET THE COMPANION
INFINITE IMPACT TOOLKIT!

This book isn't just going to share theory—it's about taking action.

This Toolkit gives you access to many of my *very best* tools, documents, and resources to more naturally achieve the desired outcomes for your books and business in a more effortless manner. Considering that organizing, documenting, and sharing crucial business information to team members, vendors, and mentors may not be your strength, this Toolkit is designed to help streamline your operations!

Some of what's included:

- **The Infinite Impact Workbook** to formally document your brand-specific avatar, vision, why, core values, and strategies so that any team member, vendor, or mentor can stay in alignment with your brand as they work to support your growth.

- **Books & Business Dashboard**—what I call the "Source of Truth" for your brand. This comprehensive spreadsheet serves as a central hub for all the links and assets within your company (from lead magnets to speaking engagements, and your customer journey to offer stack). This streamlines the sharing of information and keeps everyone on the same page.

- **Exercises Log** to enhance your book journey experience. This document offers you a clean space to journal your way through the exercises in the book.
- **Fast Access to Additional Training & Resources:**
  - Gain access to a video that teaches you how to outline a year's worth of specific and aligned marketing content in less than five minutes.
  - You'll also receive a job description to help you hire a Creative Marketing Assistant (CMA) who can assist with foundational content marketing and book launch project management.
  - Additionally, you can explore our NGNG Pricing Menu to model our strategy and layout for your own business.
  - You'll also receive my exclusive Amazon book page optimization checklist, which includes tasks most publishers won't even do for you.
  - Lastly, access my library of over 100 Books & Business tip videos.

Get free access now at InfiniteImpactBook.com/Toolkit so you are fully set up for success as we dive into the powerful concepts and strategies outlined in this book.

Contents

Introduction — 1

PART ONE · PRE-WORK

CHAPTER 1
Congruence — 27

CHAPTER 2
Resistance — 39

CHAPTER 3
The Courage to Course-Correct — 59

CHAPTER 4
Alignment — 83

PART TWO · THE WORK

CHAPTER 5
Avatar — 97

CHAPTER 6
Vision — 119

CHAPTER 7
Why 147

CHAPTER 8
Values 179

PART THREE · BOOKS & BUSINESS OPTIMIZATION

CHAPTER 9
Books 201

CHAPTER 10
Business 217

CHAPTER 11
Strategy 241

PART FOUR · SCALE YOUR IMPACT

CHAPTER 12
Infinite Impact 261

Acknowledgments 273

About the Author 285

INTRODUCTION

"Hey Amber… Why do you think you're soooo busy?" asked my new mentor, Ken.

It was the winter of 2019 and I was frustrated, watching my friends "scale up" while I kept hitting a growth ceiling just beneath $1 million annually.

It was less about my colleagues, and even less about the profit potential. My angst was more about the number of lives I sensed I was destined to Impact. And…something felt off. I was experienced enough in business to know it was time to call in some outside help. That's when Ken appeared, and my journey of deep self-discovery began.

"I'm busy because I want to help as many people as possible," I replied. "I love going to bed each night exhausted, knowing I've put it all on the line and met my potential that day." I felt proud of my answer.

"Okee," Ken said.

I knew there was a vast, divine wisdom behind Ken's flannel shirt and kind eyes. He didn't share why he asked that question, or what he saw in me (that I clearly didn't see in myself). He just changed topics and the mentoring session continued.

I've thought about that question thousands of times since then.

<u>I now understand that I was "so busy" in order to hide my resistance to the spotlight. My resistance was hiding a Universe of beliefs, fears, emotions, and truths that I didn't even consciously know were creating blind spots, self-sabotaging behavior, and conflict.</u>

When I left that conversation with Ken, all I knew was that I felt curious. I had opened Pandora's box. In the following three years, I uncovered just how much I needed to work through. It was a very painful but equally gratifying time. As I started to wake up to what was holding me back, the answer seemed so obvious, as if it had been staring me in the face for years.

I was out of Alignment.

This meant I was (unknowingly) living in a way that was not in line with my deepest values and beliefs.

Although my business was still successful, it was no wonder I kept hitting that growth ceiling. I was getting in my own way.

By spending so much time in the great outdoors throughout my life, I have observed that nature operates in brilliant harmony. It balances the fight for survival with an equal measure of beauty. It was time for me to bring that same wisdom into my own life and business, by quieting my mind and engaging in the natural process of metamorphosis to bring myself back into Alignment.

The big question then became…if I was creating so much Impact while being *out* of Alignment, what could happen if I was completely in Alignment, properly discerning, and making excellent decisions?

As I worked through the roots of my resistance, not only did my business break through the growth ceiling, but I was also able to innovate "The Work" (my Foundational Four Framework—an unconventional and modernized approach to the mainstream business pillars of Avatar, Vision, Why, and Values) necessary for my clients to overcome their resistance as well.

This book reveals pertinent parts of my story and many valuable strategies and lessons I've learned to help you fast-track your success through your own Books & Business journey.

Your mission is to get your Avatar, Vision, Why, and Values working harmoniously in your (current or upcoming) Books & Business platform so that you can achieve the Impact that's in your heart to make. We'll be unpacking exactly how to do that the rest of our time together.

In Chapter 1, we'll begin by measuring your current state of congruence—operational harmony—to identify any blind spots we can repair. We start here because:

- → When a company is operating out of Alignment, the leader will unknowingly make decisions that negatively impact bottom-line results.
- → When the leader makes Aligned decisions, and their Books & Business operate harmoniously, congruence is achieved and Impact ripples out to degrees beyond what they can imagine.

Knowing your starting point—how well-Aligned you are (or not)—will prepare you for The Work to come.

So, let me pose the same question that began my journey to you: **Why are *you* so busy?**

Yes, you are busy trying to be and do the best you can. <u>And…this question also begs accountability for what you're resisting</u>:

- Is there a book in you (or several) that sits on your computer in draft mode?
- Do you resist recording videos or being consistent with your social media marketing?
- What have you been putting off, waiting for the "right" time?

If you're anything like the thousands of authors and entrepreneurs I've worked with for nearly 20 years, there's a good chance you're experiencing resistance in at least one of these areas. While I'll dive into the details of my personal journey in the chapters to come, this book is also an invitation for you to look inside—to examine your own journey and what has kept you from making the Impact you are committed to making in the world. For now, the important thing to note is that I had been hitting a growth ceiling because…

==I was in resistance (which really meant I was unknowingly hiding from being seen or heard).==

For more than 15 years of my business journey, I strictly focused my attention on being in service to others. I strategically designed ways to hide safely to the side of the spotlight. (Nothing to see here, folks!) My following was growing, the raves were pouring in, word of mouth had more than taken care of the business, and I had a long list of accomplishments. Great, right? Yes, and… I was in a constant state of overdrive (approval-seeking), and I was burning out.

"Just stay busy. One foot in front of the other. No one needs to know I'm shelving the fifth version of the book I've been trying to write for a decade, or that I'm making non-stop excuses to my team as to why I can't execute on certain projects 'right now.' The public doesn't need to know that I'm learning how to be a single mom. No one needs to know just how exhausted I am from living incongruently. Best to hide the fact that the biggest trauma of my life is happening as we hit the prestigious Inc. 5000 business award, a glorious moment for any business owner. One foot in front of the other. Just stay busy."

We can have a genuine experience of success AND have secret thoughts and feelings inside that self-sabotage our opportunity to play full out with our lives. Both can be true and exist at the same time.

You see, for me, there was always some justified reason why I had to shelve the next version of my book. Initially, a ghostwriter I'd hired couldn't seem to get the depth and breadth of my work. A year and a half later, after starting again, "life happened" and I had to hit the pause button on writing because it just wasn't the right time. Then a year later, a writing partner had significant delays due to challenges in his personal life. Nearly two years later, a ghostwriter I'd hired was way off base and wasn't presenting my content or voice in a way that felt congruent. There was always a reason why I couldn't move forward.

The incompleteness of projects was my clue that something was off. (After all, if my true Aligned passion was activated, there would be no question about prompt completion and strong forward momentum…)

For clients, I've seen them push back their release date because of busyness, a need for more editing, or a sudden shift in business priorities. I've watched as they delayed the launch of their monetization model we'd spent months building out or decided not to proceed altogether at the one-yard line because of a new idea they wanted to pursue instead. These are all clues pointing to their own resistance—blind spots taking them down.

We are each at risk of these setbacks. But year after year, we must own up to the obvious pattern. If we ever want to know what we are truly capable of with the time we have left in life, it is high time we dig into the resistance now, and not wait.

In my personal journey, it was ONLY when I leaned in and did The Work that I saw just how out of Alignment I had been.

THE WORK
FOUNDATIONAL FOUR FRAMEWORK

Avatar:

- → Traditional approach: A representation of potential customers (allows for multiple personas to make up an audience of buyers).
- → AmberV's perspective: The one person you are in service of, in every action you take.
- → What's the difference? When you speak to an audience of multiple personas, your message lands in a more general way. It's far more congruent and effective to speak to one person and be fully self-expressed.

Vision:

- → Traditional approach: A written statement that describes a company's purpose and long-term goals.
- → AmberV's perspective: What you consciously choose to spend your life in service of, on an individual level, for the benefit of humanity.
- → What's the difference? Instead of focusing on your global impact (which can often feel unreachable), I propose you go deep and define exactly how you would like to help one person at a time.

Why:

- → Traditional approach: A written statement that describes a company's purpose and mission.
- → AmberV's perspective: What you receive in exchange for dedicating your life to the pursuit of your Vision.
- → What's the difference? I propose mutual reciprocation in the relationship between Vision and Why. *This was a game-changer for me!*

Values:

- → Traditional approach: The principles and standards of behavior that guide a company's decision-making and actions.
- → AmberV's perspective: A set of root principles by which you choose to guide and live your life.
- → What's the difference? I propose you commit your values to memory and use them as the language of the organization. The differentiation lies in how we use them as a powerful tool in life and business.

Your Avatar, Vision, Why, and Values must be clearly and honestly defined in order to achieve Alignment

Note: major life events or significant personal growth may require a re-Alignment of these pillars.

When I met Ken, I thought my Avatar, Vision, Why, and Values were clear and true. What surprised me was that in the process of getting curious about and shifting my resistance, I changed. <u>And as I changed, my Why changed and needed to be redefined</u>.

While my Avatar, Vision, Why, and Values hadn't changed in many years, the business started to fracture because I was no longer in Alignment with my Why.

I sensed something was off because projects weren't getting completed, and I didn't know how to locate the blind spot that was causing this. *(Can you relate?)*

I continued to hesitate and resist, waiting to get clarity (…years passing by…). Furthermore, I hadn't yet integrated my team with my Foundational Four, so they couldn't see how to protect the Alignment of the organization either.

Only when I went through the exercise I'll walk you through in Chapter 3 did I discover that I was unknowingly hiding. My blind spot was finally revealed. I hadn't been able to finish my book because *I wasn't truly ready to be seen or heard*. I was resistant to the very things I knew I needed to do to use my voice and make a far greater Impact. Only once I did The Work and redefined my Why did I find myself in Alignment. A new passion for this project was awakened within me, and the entire book poured out of me in just over two months (with no ghostwriter) because I was finally Aligned and operating in congruence.

We are all humans, having one heck of a human experience. **No one is exempt, and that is why this is no place for judgment or shaming (of each other, or ourselves).**

This book is a call to action to come out from hiding behind your busyness, to get in Alignment, and to be fully self-expressed so that your Impact ripples out stronger than ever.

HOW WE CREATE INFINITE IMPACT

Before we go any further, I want you to think of someone you had a strong Impact on.

It could be at any point in your journey; it could be a public act of heroism or an exchange that only one other person knew about. There is no qualifier here. Consider someone you think of fondly, knowing your words/actions/presence/love made a difference. Hold that person's face and name in your mind.

Now imagine that person—who is forever changed—moving forward and living their life differently. You inherently changed them for the better. Imagine they pay it forward (perhaps unknowingly) by impacting each person they encounter for the rest of their life. It all started with you. *Doesn't that feeling make you come alive?*

It might come more naturally for you to think instead about someone who had a significant Impact on your life. Consider how you behaved differently after your time with them, or think of their words of wisdom that you've shared with others countless times…. This is what Infinite Impact is all about.

Infinite Impact is possible when we harness our focus and energy to create a meaningful and memorable Impact with each individual we come across.

That effort results in a lasting feeling each individual embodies after an encounter with us that changes who they are and the course of their journey, and is then shared naturally with each individual they encounter, effectively spreading our Impact into infinity.

This book invites us all (myself included) to move through fear and discomfort to make an Impact anyway. To make that phone call even though we had a hard day and just want to hide. To publish that book even though we are afraid of the feedback and what that means for our future. To extend kindness to strangers, even though the world can sometimes make us feel defeated.

YOUR STRATEGIC GUIDE TO BOOKS & BUSINESS SUCCESS

Once we have an opportunity to identify our own areas of incongruence in Chapter 1, we will begin the repair process with a quest to uncover things we misinterpreted from our past (generally due to our young age and not fully understanding most of what happened to us or why). These misinterpretations become beliefs that then create resistance and incongruence (what occurs when we are out of Alignment).

What is even more interesting than the stories we tell ourselves is the meaning we assign to them. Our mission is to get curious about those memories and shift the beliefs we formed around them so they are no longer life-taking, and instead become life-giving. We will work through this process of examining our memories and shifting our beliefs in **Chapters 2-3** so that we will be ready to be seen and heard, get in Alignment (as discussed in **Chapter 4**), and make our Impact on the world while we still have time.

I will support you step-by-step through The Work (Avatar, Vision, Why, and Values) in **Chapters 5-8** and can almost guarantee you've not experienced these company pillars in the way I'm going to teach them. This is how you'll get in Alignment, whether for the first time or once again after a major life change. Either way, it is a moment to celebrate fully. *(And we could start celebrating our wins a bit more, don't you think?)*

NOW WHAT THE HECK DOES THIS HAVE TO DO WITH BOOKS & BUSINESS?

For nearly two decades, authors and entrepreneurs like you have been coming to me saying, "I want to publish a book and help people." I call this The Author's Hero's Journey.

You have the right idea here because launching a great book is the fastest way to scale your Impact.

Most think it's as easy as:

1. Build an online platform *(branding, website, social channels, initial offer stack)*
2. Launch my book(s)
3. Make an Impact

You've heard the phrase, "If it were that easy, everyone would be doing it"? Well, many authors have built a platform and launched it, but it certainly wasn't easy, and 99% of the time it didn't get them the sales, prestige, or Impact they wanted.

Did you know the average author sells less than 300 books over the lifetime of the title?!

I've talked with authors who were on *The Today Show* and sold less than 50 books from the show's debut. *(The Today Show!)*

It's not uncommon for a business owner to invest $50,000-200,000 in the build-out of their platform and launch of their first book, only to turn around and sell a few hundred copies at most, leaving the author feeling like they made a terrible decision in pursuing their dream. This is completely unacceptable to me!

Authors have lost extreme amounts of money, time, and confidence because of one critical missing piece in their formula: they didn't know how to get into — and more so, stay in! — Alignment. Further, they didn't know how to apply their uniqueness to the best Books & Business strategies in the industry.

You may not realize (or even believe) that this internal work needs to be done to achieve a high degree of Impact beyond just building your platform and launching your book. Or, perhaps you've already done a measure of The Work thus far but still feel like you're missing something.

I'll tell you this, friend…in my nearly 20 years as a Books & Business strategist working with authors at every stage of business, from startups to multi-million-dollar brands, <u>I know the further you go into growing your online platform and nearing that book release date, your resistance and lack of mental and emotional preparedness will be exposed, and it will threaten not just your launch but also your ability to make long-term Impact</u>. We can't let that happen!

That's why doing The Work has to come first. **If you skip doing The Work to get in Alignment, you'll be unprepared to handle the attention when it hits.** The outcome? It looks and feels like a really harsh wake-up call. This is usually when an entrepreneur is left with a bad reputation or is forced to scale down and recalibrate.

Once you are in Alignment, I can rock your world with **Books & Business strategy**, operations, and best practices so you operate in full congruence moving forward. That's what **Chapters 9-11** will cover, and this is where your reading experience will pick up a lot of speed and momentum!

In **Chapter 9**, I'm going to break down the 6 Phases of a book launch that have been extremely effective for the authors we serve. In fact, they are so effective that my company became known as one of the top book launch and business growth companies in America. And, as a companion to this book, you'll get special access to my **Books & Business Toolkit** (found at www.InfiniteImpactBook.com) that contains SOPs, templates, instructional videos, and training, so you get a huge leg up for your next launch!

It's in the book launch phase that authors have the greatest potential to dip in and out of some pretty heavy resistance. *(This is when your future self will be forever grateful that you did The Work, which you may initially feel is unnecessary.)*

As you "sell yourself," rally your community around your cause, ask for support, and are seen and heard more than ever before… disempowering emotions grow, sowing seeds of doubt. The mind starts routing an escape plan, and your possibility for Infinite Impact is threatened, along with all of the time and money you've invested up to that point. This book and the framework herein give you awareness and guidance to move around those land mines.

In **Chapters 10 and 11**, get ready for a deep dive into marketing, sales, and operations. I share the nitty-gritty details of the small adjustment I made in my business to bring in the following **sales results**:

- → Cut my sales call time spent by 50%.
- → Eliminated sales-pitch jitters.
- → Experienced significant time savings as 95% of prospects who schedule a call now are qualified buyers.
- → Improved my closing percentage from 25% to 60%+, which greatly grew my confidence.
- → Doubled our profit.

In the same chapter, I then share the one simple strategy I deployed that continued to get me these **marketing results**:

- → Too many qualified leads. (Yep, after less than one year of my team consistently implementing a new marketing operation, I had to stop because it was too successful. #PositiveProblem.)
- → Greater company protection by keeping operations in-house vs. being beholden to an agency.

→ Significant cost savings in three critical areas of the business.

→ I cut my personal time spent on marketing activities by 90%. Freedom, baby!

As you witness my results, you'll see with great clarity how you can also naturally attract and convert more qualified buyers to your business, grow your profit, and scale your Impact through developing meaningful connection with others.

THE IMPORTANCE OF TEAM

As we address the concept of team, I classify my clients in one of two categories:

- Those who identify as a "solopreneur" with no team.
- Those who have a team, regardless of size.

I've largely found that **solopreneurs** actually have a team, but they don't identify them that way for whatever reason. A solopreneur might work with a freelance ghostwriter, editor, mentor, or lawyer. They may be contracted with a social media or paid ads agency, CRM specialist, or web designer. Believe it or not, your team is comprised of ALL the people who support the decision-making and execution of your business activities. They don't need to be employees to be connected to you and your cause.

The problem is that since you haven't identified them as your team, they don't have the guidance and information necessary (from The Work) to do a phenomenal job for you. When lackluster results inevitably ensue, you might be quick to blame the team member; however, more often than not, you didn't give them what they needed to be successful in the first place. And that's when you get disheartened and perhaps grow resistant to the idea of growing a team to begin with. I'll do my best to change your mindset on this.

Your team includes any individual who:

- **Supports your decision-making** such as an Executive Assistant, COO, Mentor, Coach, Strategist, Creative Marketing Assistant (CMA), Lawyer, etc., and/or
- **Has any degree of influence over your brand and content** such as your web designer, social media coordinator, podcast producer, funnel builder, paid ads or SEO (Search Engine Optimization) expert, etc.

Over the years, I've closely consulted with business owners ranging from solopreneurs to CEOs running a 200+ employee firm. **All** of these leaders faced some degree of challenge regarding their team. There is resistance on both sides of the fence. (Even with all of the business and leadership books and programs on the market, there is so much work to be done in this area to bridge the communication and congruence gap.)

I am a strong advocate for you having a small team who can help you stay in Alignment and effectively take tasks off your plate to further protect your time and energy. After all, your focus should be on using your voice and making an Infinite Impact.

The key to working with your team (which I will help you do throughout the course of this book) is to let them see behind the curtain and into the heart of your Avatar, Vision, Why, and Values. They also need proper training and guidance to get stuff done for you, which is what I will be providing for them throughout this book.

This book is meant to be experienced with your team—EACH member of your team as defined above—because it is unlikely that you will stay in Alignment if you are alone in trying to uphold the standard.

If you are one of the few entrepreneurs who legitimately have no team, then I strongly suggest you hire at least one part-time assistant to support your workload. I call this person a **Creative Marketing Assistant (CMA for short—remember this term!)**. In your Books & Business Toolkit, I even give you a job description for this role, plus offer resources to hire and train this individual!

A CMA is a perfect first hire for any business and a general requirement I have for my consulting clients. Moving forward on our journey together, I will assume that you will get this (or related) hire under your belt as quickly as possible so that they can support you as you implement the action steps in this book. I've taken it upon myself to protect your time and energy—so much so that I've built my company offerings around the idea of getting at least one team member to support you.

If you already have a team, then great! You're one step ahead of the game, and you'll find the concepts in the book that much faster to implement.

Either way, you'll love this... Throughout the book, in relevant chapters, you'll see "Team Action List" prompts. That's their queue to move the concepts in the book forward inside your company walls so you experience progress right away.

By sending each team member (including vendors) a copy of the book, they can read along with you in a weekly company book club, or on their own to anticipate your needs. A whole-team approach will also protect your Alignment long-term (how nice does that sound?).

In the team sections, I even advise them to bring forward certain discussion topics as you head into quarterly and annual meetings to take more pressure off of you. I've outlined accountability structures *(that you don't have to manage)* that will give you the best chance of succeeding long-term with the strategies outlined in this book. All guidance will be listed at the end of relevant chapters.

HOW TO GET THE MOST OUT OF THIS BOOK

This isn't a book to put down and come back to when you "have more time."

Remember what "being busy" got me? Stuck. I want nothing more than for you to take immediate action and see progress with every step.

Here are some quick notes on how I encourage you to interact with this book:

- You don't have to strain to understand and implement every concept in the whole book the first time through. Be comfortable with picking up only what is needed for you at this stage of your journey, and rest assured, there is always more here for you in the future.
    - Additionally, note that the chapters do build off of one another. I won't stop you from skipping to the Business chapters (or even scoping out the ending next), but please know that, to get maximum results, I encourage you to stay focused and disciplined by reading the book and doing the exercises from beginning to end without taking too many breaks between chapters.
- This book is designed to be experienced with the companion **Books & Business Toolkit** to get maximum results from

the content. (Go to www.InfiniteImpactBook.com and get access now.) Again, it's a bundle of my best SOPs, templates, instructional videos, and training, so you get full support in designing your customer journey and annual content plan, upgrading your website, rocking your social media, launching your book, and beyond.

- As an additional companion, please consider joining my Books & Business membership (details also found at www.InfiniteImpactBook.com) where you'll be in a safe space with like-minded, Values-Aligned entrepreneurs. I'll use the guiding principles in this book to give you targeted strategies and best practices each month.

- I'm going to suggest that you **review the exercises in this book annually with your team** to ensure you are staying in Alignment as life piles on its new challenges, setbacks, and distractions. Mark a date on your calendar next year (you'll likely have new team members on board who can join you) to complete round two.

- I suggest you mark this book up as you dive into the exercises. Go to town. Highlight, underline, write comments, earmark, record your answers to writing prompts, add post-its, and more. Some of the stories and calls to action may confront you or stir the pot a little bit. When that happens, just remember that the challenge is the opportunity. This is a safe space to be honest with yourself about what's not working and what you'd rather experience instead. That kind of honesty is *necessary* to get the results you know are possible for your life.

- Lastly, I hope you share this book with others you know who could use it. No one can do the journey alone. In fact, this book comes out of my Core Value that we are better together. Consider **starting a Mastermind with peers** and use the principles in this book as a jumping-off point for deep, productive discussion. (If you reach out to me, I may even team up with you to help monetize this idea.) Be the leader who helps others experience their own version of Infinite Impact. This will bring you deep fulfillment.

By now, if you're listening to that voice inside—your intuition—there should be a gentle nudge. Something that could almost be mistaken for hesitation or uncertainty.

It's not anything you should be concerned about…

It's a deep calling for your significance to come out and play.

That nudge is an indicator that something in this introduction resonated (felt true) with you. Accountability was experienced.

You are being called forward.

I urge you to take a step into the unknown because that's where your greatest Impact is waiting for you. Your life is ready for more meaning, more joy, and more fulfillment. It is my great honor to share with you all that I've learned as I leaned in and faced my scariest fears to deliver this work to you.

BOTTOM LINE, IF YOU ARE...

- *Sick and tired* of not making serious progress building your following/profit/Impact...
- *Sick and tired* of feeling defeated, stuck, and exhausted from trying to "do it all" yourself...
- *Sick and tired* of investing tens of thousands of dollars and countless wasted hours on products, programs, and memberships that only teach you "part" of the solution, leaving you feeling overwhelmed and full of regret...
- *Sick and tired* of not using your gifts and talents in the way you know you could if you JUST had the right help...the right plan...the right combination of elements...

If you're sick and tired of any (or all) of those things, this book is exactly what you have been waiting for.

Let's now move forward together to uncover your resistance, gain the Courage to Course-Correct, define and achieve Alignment, and be fully self-expressed with your Books & Business—operating in congruence so you can create an Impact on the world that will ripple out infinitely...

"They tried to bury us.
They didn't know we were seeds."
- Dinos Christianopoulos

PART ONE

PRE-WORK

CHAPTER 1
CONGRUENCE

Are You Ready to Make an Infinite Impact?

"I want to start a business and launch a book to help people. It's not even about the money; it's more about the impact I want to have."

This is what many people say when they come to me for strategic planning and implementation support. (And btw, I LOVE that.)

My question is ... how does someone know they are worthy of their cause and ready to make a significant Impact?

Going through years of pain, gain, confusion, loneliness, achievement, and suffering reveals "your cause" and makes you worthy to a large degree. But it's not the full equation.

This question challenges whether you are *ready* to go all in on advocating for your cause in a responsible way so that you achieve maximum Impact in not just your lifetime, but for generations to come.

Being worthy of a cause is the result of competence, conviction, readiness for advocacy, and earned trust from your community—the full embodiment of leadership that makes you deserving of representing that cause.

You see, Alignment is achieved by doing The Work (Aligning your Avatar, Vision, Why, and Values in the unique ways I teach them). But there is another part to the equation. You must select and follow through on customized Books & Business strategies that are in Alignment so your entire business operates harmoniously.

==Therefore, worthiness is the prize for operating in congruence.==

Millions of authors are (unintentionally, but…) ***irresponsibly*** rushing to market and slapping generic content out to the world hoping to help people, yet they haven't done The Work to properly prepare. They're not ready. The outcome is a dud of a book, and a social media channel that looks and sounds like everyone else, and when they don't get the results they hoped for, they experience a whole lot of emotional baggage to boot.

If this sounds familiar, it's partly out of a hidden fear of being seen and heard (this is when resistance shows up and what we'll be tackling head-on in Chapter 2), and partly because you're in a rush and want to take action while you're motivated to do so.

When will the standard be raised?

When will we take our Vision and preparation more seriously?

How much more time will pass before we courageously move forward and play full out the way we were uniquely shaped to do by our life experiences?

You can't expect to make it big in the NFL just because you threw around a football in the backyard as a kid. You need to:

- Train—and train HARD.
- Condition your body to be the ultimate machine that can weather the impact and intensity of the games.
- Seek out a lot of strong coaching to optimize your mindset, channel your focus, stay disciplined, and prepare for the win.
- Lean on the unbreakable bond of your teammates to push you way farther than you could ever go alone.

- Demonstrate unwavering clarity of your Vision, who you're doing this for, and Why.
- Be all-in, fully Aligned, and ready to maximize your potential.

There are no shortcuts. You can't buy your way in.

You earn the respect of the fans through hard work, showing up, and winning time and time again. You earn their love because of how fiercely you give to them each minute that you play.

If you want to play at the highest levels, and Impact to the fullest degree, you must do The Work to prepare. *You must follow a specific process so you are ready for your spotlight moment instead of fumbling on the one-yard line like so many good-hearted individuals have done before you.*

<u>This book isn't going to just share theory. This book is about taking action</u>.

It doesn't matter if you are a startup or have been in business for more than a decade, we'll begin by taking a snapshot—an accounting of how ready you are to make an Infinite Impact. Next, we'll get you in Alignment so you operate in congruence moving forward.

CONGRUENCE ASSESSMENT

Before we begin, keep in mind that doing The Work is a deep and soulful journey that requires a high degree of self-reflection and vulnerability. The more honesty you bring to this exercise, the more likely you are to experience life-changing results as you move through the rest of the book.

Instructions:

- Carefully reflect back on your personal/professional experiences, then select the number from 1-5 that best describes your usual mindset or pattern of behavior, and write it in the space provided.
- When your tendency is to answer "3 - Neutral," explore past experiences to see if you lean more toward "2 - Disagree" or "4 - Agree."
- <u>Team-related questions</u>: If you are a solopreneur with no active contractor or vendor relationships supporting you, answer "3 - Neutral."

> 5 - Strongly Agree   4 - Agree   3 - Neutral
> 2 - Disagree   1 - Strongly Disagree

1. I know my Core Values so completely that I naturally use them when making important decisions about my life and business. _____

2. When meeting new people, I feel fully open and present, ready to make an Impact at that moment. *(Rather than feeling guarded or reserved, waiting for others to come to me.)* _____

3. When I look at photos of myself, watch myself on video, or listen to myself in an interview or on a podcast, I feel confident in what I have to say. *(As opposed to avoiding these things, experiencing negative self-talk, and/or finding flaws in my presentation.)* _____

4. I know my ideal customer (Avatar) so well that I can visualize what they are thinking and feeling, moment by moment, as they go through their daily life. I also intimately know their greatest hopes and deepest insecurities and fears. _____

5. I am comfortable being seen and heard by others because I know my value in the world. _____

6. I have identified my strengths and weaknesses. My team protects me by managing and taking on the work that drains me, thereby protecting my energy and allowing me to focus on tasks that keep me in flow. _____

7. When it comes to producing content, I have a well-organized weekly content plan, a clear structure around what I want to say, and total conviction when saying it. _____

8. I often find myself speaking with others in the language of my Core Values. _____

9. I have an optimized customer journey that repeatedly and steadily converts qualified prospects into raving customers. _____

10. I am fully self-expressed in my approach to marketing, sales, and operations. *(Rather than taming or hiding my uniqueness to fit in.)* _____

11. My offer stack is congruent. I no longer create products and/or services out of "I should…" and instead embrace, "I want to, and get to…"—creating offers from a place of confidence and clarity. _____

12. It feels natural and comfortable for me to ask friends and peers to help promote my cause and/or refer me to others. _____

13. I carefully consider my Core Values and use them as a filter when hiring and/or considering new partnerships. _____

14. When people compliment or validate me, I naturally agree with and appreciate their sentiments. *(As opposed to deflecting, not fully receiving, or taking it in.)* _____

15. I have hit my stride with my ability to attract the right team members, train them effectively, and consistently give them what they need to achieve my Vision. _____

16. At work, I hold myself and those around me accountable for upholding the Core Values of the organization. _____

17. I operate in a state of playfulness and excitement. *(Rather than forcing things to get done and wrestling with the process.)* _____

18. I make intentional decisions about the experience my audience has when engaging with my brand (visually, emotionally, intellectually, etc.) because I am deeply passionate about the Vision, Why, and Core Values it represents. _____

19. I dedicate ample time every day exclusively to the practice of spreading my cause. This is non-negotiable because I know it will give me the Impact and reward I want to experience in life. _____

20. I am confident in and feel worthy of my cause. I am committed to doing The Work it takes to achieve my Vision so that I can experience the level of freedom and fulfillment that comes only as a result of going all-in. _____

YOUR TOTAL: _____

TALLY YOUR RESULTS:

90-100: I'm impressed! Take a moment to fully experience pride and gratitude because you are doing a LOT right. You are in a high state of congruence. Because of that, as you work through the exercises in the book, you'll get to focus on the more advanced optimization techniques to maximize your Impact. The key for you will be to continue to make sure your team, vendors, and strategic partners stay in Alignment with you.

80-90: Well done! We've identified that you are doing a lot of things well, and we've also identified some key areas for improvement. You'll likely experience a lot of progress as you complete the chapter exercises. By building out some processes, optimizing your natural energy levels and self-expression, plus getting your team Aligned to protect you, you'll bust through that glass ceiling for sure.

70-80: You are well on your way! Allow yourself to feel glad that you've identified some blind spots and areas for improvement. You may have instinctively known there was room for improvement, and now have a specific list of growth opportunities. That's really cool. You're about to get a lot of high-level support in the pages ahead. Complete the exercises, take notes, involve your team, and get ready for some serious positive benefits rolling your way.

60-70: This is a great start. You'll likely make some strong strides in the weeks ahead. Know that you are *fully* supported with this book, and by your team once you get them involved in this process. As we progress through the chapters and exercises, you'll learn how to put systems in place to free up your time, remove distractions, ensure you have more clarity in decision-making, bypass a lot of the trial-and-error work most people do, and rally the support of other community leaders to help amplify your cause. It's time to get more support so you can leapfrog forward into the experiences you're ready to live!

Below 60: I'm so glad we're connected and that you're here to do The Work! It's going to be a serious game-changer for you! By the time you're done reading this book and working through the exercises, you will have tremendous clarity on your goals and roadmap. You'll also know how to attract the right customers, sell and Impact at higher levels, get others to spread your cause for you, get the right team in Alignment to protect your energy, and so much more. Allow yourself to enjoy the ride of learning and growth. One day, you'll look back and feel immense pride for your willingness to do what most others won't. You've got this!

You can use your individual results as a general guide to measure your readiness for creating Infinite Impact. I recommend that you retake this assessment every six months for further accountability and evaluation of your overall progress.

If you are surprised or disappointed by your results, don't feel bad! Most people who come to me score below 60 when we first start working together. (Thank goodness we identified some of your blind spots now before you invested tens of thousands of dollars and countless hours trying to grow your brand!)

For a more accurate and detailed assessment of your current state of readiness, and to explore quick strategies to experience faster progress, you can schedule a "Readiness Consultation" with one of our team members by going to www.InfiniteImpactBook.com/Schedule.

Either way, we've now identified some of your most likely blind spots, which is great progress early in our journey. We're going to keep up this momentum to locate other hurdles that may be hiding in the shadows. The faster you face what's been getting in your way, the faster you will move beyond it and into an experience of personal freedom and fulfillment.

> "Surround yourself with only people who are going to lift you higher."
> - Oprah Winfrey

CHAPTER 2

RESISTANCE

Now that we have a baseline of where you are in the process of preparation, it's time to dig deep and make some serious progress in the next couple of chapters.

Early on the path toward making an Impact, you'll come to learn a LOT about your own inner resistance.

Resistance comes up when you know you should create a video, but *don't wanna*. You know you have to be active on social media, but you *don't wanna*. You know you should reach out to peers and ask for their support in promotion, but don't because it's hard or embarrassing or time-consuming.

There's always a good reason why you can't do these things *right now*, right?

If you're anything like me, I was just "too busy" (honest interpretation: resisting). Resistance can be *extremely helpful* as it indicates something inside we need to explore.

However, if left unaddressed, resistance expresses itself in the form of hiding, and that's when…

Resistance is poison for a dream.

Resistance sprouts out of a belief from deep inside our subconscious, and the source is almost impossible to pinpoint unless you're guided.

If you really explore your resistance in business, you'll find it present in activities where there's an increased chance of being <u>seen</u> or <u>heard</u> by yourself (ignoring your intuition) or others.

For nearly 20 years, I've witnessed firsthand the resistance in entrepreneurs who thought they were ready to make an Impact. Most would never admit it; they moved like chameleons, but to me, it was obvious.

Once I helped those leaders identify where their resistance was coming from, they were able to create a solid foundation and move forward in Alignment. And—bonus!—I'm about to walk you through an exercise to move more quickly through this piece. Once clients experienced this shift, it almost seemed like magic how effortlessly the business results started to show up for them!

WHAT RESISTANCE LOOKS AND FEELS LIKE

(Reader Note: I encourage you to reflect on the following list and check the boxes that resonate with you.)

I see resistance when people…

- ☐ Say they have a face for radio.
- ☐ Don't trust their own monetization ideas.
- ☐ Sit on the draft of their book for years.
- ☐ Regularly tinker with their brand messaging, never satisfied.
- ☐ Ask *me* what their goals should be.
- ☐ Struggle to record video, especially consistently.
- ☐ Reschedule their own webinars and events time and time again.
- ☐ Don't like the majority of (or all) photos of themselves.
- ☐ Fire yet another team member for not capturing their voice correctly.
- ☐ Have significant delays in asking their network to promote their product/program/launch.
- ☐ Are nervous to ask for testimonials or endorsements.
- ☐ Don't take decisive action, instead let overdue tasks build up.
- ☐ Ask *me* what their sales offers should be.
- ☐ Procrastinate writing emails or preparing lead magnet materials.
- ☐ Don't let any one idea live long enough to see if it could really work.
- ☐ Want a team member to do all of their social media perfectly, yet never get involved themselves.

If more than five of these sound familiar, there's work to do so you feel more comfortable being seen and heard.

When you are resistant to doing the tasks required to accomplish the very thing you want most (Impact), you must take the time to explore where that resistance is coming from and shift it to move forward more effectively.

Resistance is connected to hiding.

The majority of entrepreneurs felt "not good enough" as a kid in some way, shape, or form, and now spend their adulthood repeatedly proving that story wrong.

1. If there was a time in your childhood when you were seen or heard and something bad happened as a result, you might have misinterpreted that as not being valued—not being good enough.

2. If you have a deep-rooted fear of not being enough, you will weave in and out of hiding (avoiding tasks that run the risk of you being seen or heard) to protect yourself from not feeling valued again.

When our body senses a threat to our well-being, it responds in one of four ways:

1. **Fight** shows up as **overcompensation**: "I'll be loud about how much I know and how right I am to mask how powerless I really feel inside. If I force you to see and hear me, I'll be safe."

2. **Flight** shows up as **avoidance**: "I'll put up walls and limit access to people and situations where I'm uncomfortable or uncertain of the outcome. I want to avoid pain or rejection at all costs."

3. **Freeze** shows up as **doing nothing**: "Conflict means I am in immediate danger. This causes me to be so overwhelmed and paralyzed by fear that I literally cannot think clearly or take action."

4. **Fawn** shows up as **surrender and/or acceptance**: "If I'm seen or heard I will definitely be hurt, so I'll flatter you and give you the attention, hoping you'll decide to hurt me just a little bit less. I give away my power." (Cough, cough.)

The problem with these trauma responses? It is incredibly draining over a long period of time to be anything other than your true, authentic self with others. Your self-made protection will keep your Impact small and leave you feeling dissatisfied. You'll be tortured knowing you are capable of more, but ultimately, your blind spots and fear will continue to keep you stuck.

In my experience, resistance meant I would:

- Severely overthink my content. I published valuable content consistently, but certain deeper, more vulnerable work got shelved.

- Leave my marketing team hanging out to dry because I was "too busy" to give them certain types of content.
- Decline certain speaking engagements or opportunities because I secretly felt insecure about my own expertise or performance quality. I blamed it on being an introvert.

Did you notice the overuse of the word "certain" there?

That's because **I would weave in and out of resistance like a true pro.**

I did "just enough" of everything to stay under the radar. The inability to use my authentic *(fully self-expressed)* voice to share my deeper wisdom, and a tendency to push others to be seen and chosen ahead of me, turned out to be themes that carried through many relationships and experiences I had well into adulthood. After all, as a kid, I learned that when I stuck my neck out too far (being seen or heard), a bad outcome was headed my way.

One of the reasons we are so blind to the roots of our resistance is because they took seed in our childhood. When we were young, we misinterpreted much about the world around us. Our core beliefs came from a time when we didn't have a clear perspective on what was unfolding.

By exploring what we misinterpreted, we can quickly shift into a state of courage that will give us the power to knock out any task (while enjoying the ride) and experience our true significance.

In the beginning, **most of my resistance wasn't even a conscious awareness.**

As I shared in the introduction, Ken's question about my busyness initially surprised me but kept probing me long after our call ended. I was aware that I was not operating in a natural and sustainable way, but what I didn't know was *why* I was hiding.

As I neared 40 years old, I developed an obsessive curiosity with wanting to know the truth behind my resistance. After all, I would never experience the Impact I believed I was capable of if I didn't get into Alignment, and that could never happen unless I stopped hiding away the more honest parts of myself. Those blind spots needed to reveal themselves, and promptly!

What was I hiding from?

To start, I'll breathe in courage and share that for much of my life, I didn't know who to trust or what to believe was true. That's a natural result of being told I should feel something different than what I felt, for getting in trouble for things I didn't do, or hearing that what I experienced wasn't true. There wasn't one juicy story that created my deep-rooted lack of self-trust; there were dozens.

My mom was raised in a very traumatic environment in backwoods West Virginia. I feel rage and pain every time I think about what she was forced to endure. It ultimately robbed me of the close and connected experience I craved with her.

She divorced my dad when I was 5 to embark on her spiritual journey, determined to reclaim her life. I saw firsthand how hard she worked as a single mom, and all she asked in return was that I respect her, make nice with my older sister, and keep the house clean. As a 6-year-old, all I wanted to do was make her proud, so I thought it best to take on the role of her biggest fan and protector. She needed me, and I needed her. (Win-win.) Sign me up!

Making nice with my older sister proved impossible. All I wanted was someone to play with and help take care of me. All she wanted was alone time with Mom, or space from me. But since Mom asked me to make nice, I thought it was best to keep trying. That looked like continuing to ask to play no matter how many door-slams I endured, and jogging alongside her as she briskly walked to our elementary school (...she couldn't hear me begging her to slow down, after all). Mom didn't need to know how rejected I felt at the end of most days. My job was to protect her. And yet, boy, did the hammer come down when my sister told on me for being in her room or bothering her. She was the resident star child, and I got punished.

Guilt and shame seemed to haunt my mom her whole life (...and now that I'm being honest with myself, I can admit it was really difficult to watch). As a little kid, I certainly didn't want to make it worse. She was more than just my primary caregiver. I put her on a grand pedestal as the person who showed me the most love. She was my hero for that. This was especially important to me because back then, I could count the number of people who were a significant part of my life on one hand.

Any time I would feel anger start to well up inside me as a 6-, 7-, 8-year-old kid, I locked it away in a box deep inside myself. I believed that my mom deserved better than for me to bug her about how desperately I wished I could see her more, or how much sadness, insecurity, and confusion I felt from being such an outcast at school. I believed that for the few minutes I'd get quality one-on-one time with her, it was best to be grateful and make her feel good for the choices she made in prioritizing work, travel, helping others, exercising, or escaping to the movies to unwind. That was how to keep my world as peaceful as possible. And so she knew my devotion, she would always come home to a love note from me sitting on her bedside that reminded her how amazing she was.

As I grew older, I unknowingly gave my power (and discernment abilities) to narcissists. They offered the illusion of protection and love, as long as I bent to their will.

I'd occasionally stick my neck out to take a stand and do what I felt was the right thing. The outcomes boomeranged back to me and left me far more hurt and scared. Instead, I learned how to hide my observations and limit using my voice. It was safer to not be seen or heard too much.

(Of course, I had no understanding that without being seen and heard, one doesn't feel very valuable. I had no idea how insecure I'd become underneath my invisible armor.)

For most of my life, I naturally accepted responsibility, punishment, and/or shame for many things that weren't my fault. From a young age, I believed I should. I suffered greatly and quietly.

Eventually, my outlet was to focus on finding ways to help as many kind-hearted people as I could find through my career. As I performed cartwheels and backflips for them through my company's service list, most reciprocated with appreciation. It felt like pure, cold water on a hot desert day. It was enough of a vacation from how I felt outside of work that I piled on the workload, hoping to have more joyful days

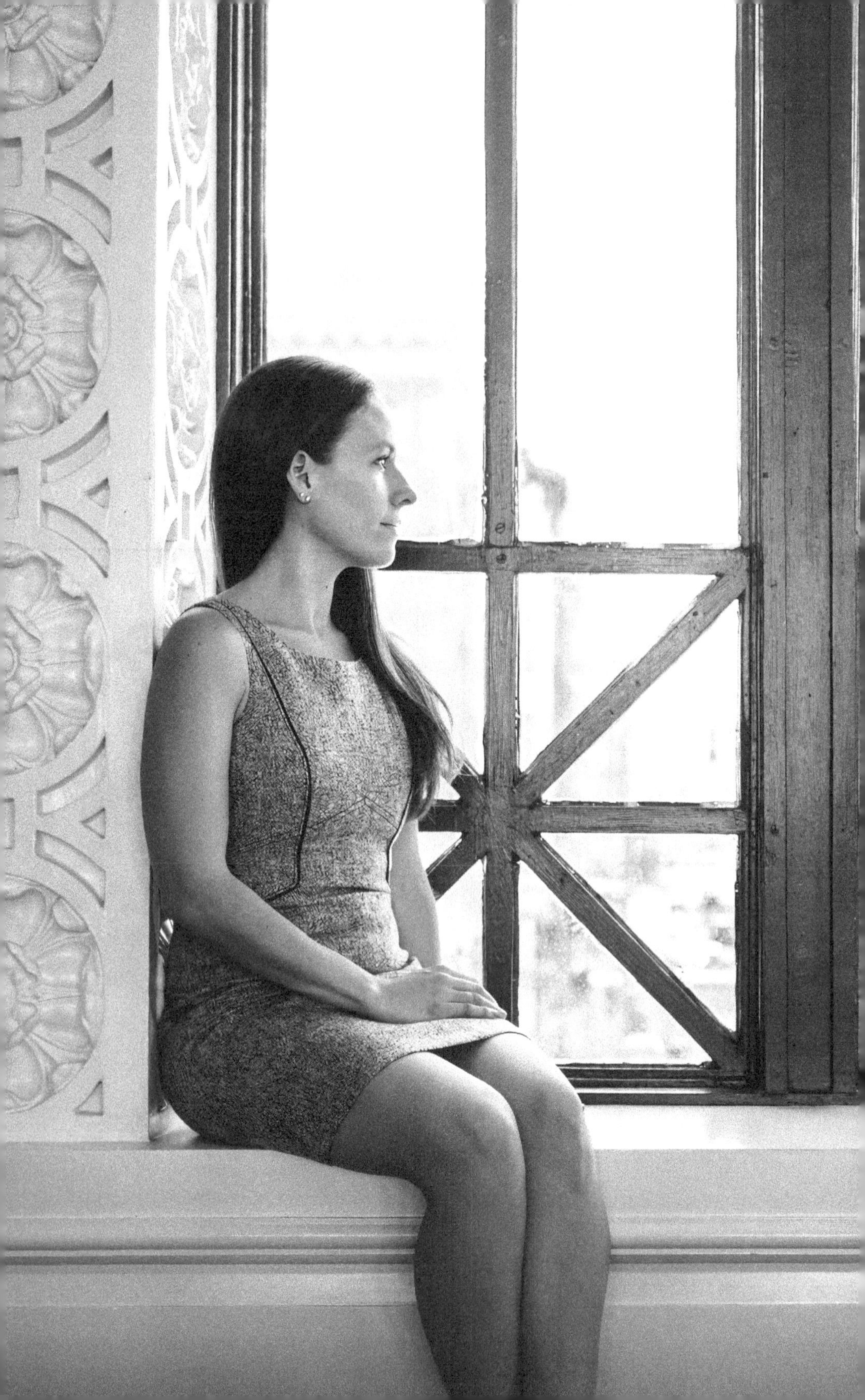

than defeating ones. I stayed busy, naming it a win-win in my mind. That is until Ken prompted my wake-up call.

If this sounds familiar to you at all, I hope it offers you comfort knowing you're not alone, but also helps you consider the roots of your own resistance as I share mine.

As mentioned above, there wasn't just one juicy story that created my deep-rooted lack of self-trust; there were dozens. And during my wake-up call season, I explored them all. After all, I was sick and tired of my blind spots cutting off my potential.

In a deep dive into my past, driven purely by curiosity, I circled back to a story I've referred to on podcasts and stages as my rock bottom moment. Even though I thought I'd healed from it fully, by revisiting it again through the frame of my resistance, it helped me not only innovate a brand-new healing and empowerment process (which I call The Courage To Course-Correct), but it also helped me see the degree to which I was hiding my voice (my truth). I clearly saw what was holding me back, and now this exercise helps me every time I sense resistance lurking in the shadows trying to sabotage my Impact-driven mindset. (This is a BIG freaking deal for me, and will soon be for you too!)

<u>I'll share the story below, and then in the following chapter, I'll walk you through "The Courage to Course-Correct" process that enabled me to overcome the resistance that I had built up from experiences like this.</u> Get cozy.

The story illustrates a time when I dared to take a stand for something I believed in and got smacked—hard. This experience was so traumatic that for decades I hid a large part of myself (out of self-protection), which is time I'll never get back. Only when I had the awareness and courage to revisit the misinterpreted memory could I unlock the tremendous gift waiting for me on the other side.

I was 16 years old when I consciously decided to go all in and share my voice. My truth.

As I've shared above, there was a laundry list of good reasons why I didn't speak up as a kid. Additionally, I didn't know how to make friends, so my entire experience of school was one of the quiet girl being the outcast. I felt confused and sad and chose to hide inside myself more, which made me more misunderstood and less and less liked. Bullying ensued throughout middle and high school, which created more feelings of suppression and isolation.

At 16, I was entangled in a whole lot of drama with a group of very unconscious and dangerous "friends." These were people I felt "good enough" to be around. My feelings of loneliness and rejection compounded so much over my younger years that I completely lacked confidence and self-worth. I hung around with anyone who would have me.

One day, my friend Dana told me a secret, which she made me swear to take to my grave. She was sleeping with my friend Ayla's boyfriend… and laughing about it.

I hated being in the car with her at that moment. It made me sick to my stomach. Yet I felt stuck. Being here was still better than being alone.

Ayla was a sweet girl—nothing like Dana who was intense and, frankly, scary to me. She didn't deserve to be betrayed like this.

I sat with the secret for days. I watched as Ayla would profusely express her undying love for her boyfriend. She wanted to marry him someday. She was so happy—the kind of happy where you're practically skipping to class because your life has certainty and meaning. I'd never experienced that personally, just on the sidelines watching her. I was so happy for her that she could achieve something I was so clueless about.

At that time, I didn't think happiness was in the cards for me (...not in a self-loathing way, just in a sort of weird acceptance because if it hadn't happened in some way by age 16, maybe it wouldn't ever happen).

I felt a *strong* internal nudge. It was one of the strongest nudges of my life. My intuition said, "Tell her."

So, the next day during our lunch break, I told Ayla the secret Dana had shared with me.

Not only did she completely reject this information (I wasn't heard), but she unfriended me and joined the others in school who had been bullying me for years.

That night, I got a scathing call from Dana. From the second I heard her voice, I gripped the phone with fear. My head got hot, my hands were trembling, and it felt like my legs were giving out. Holding onto years of trauma around punishment, I was honestly terrified of what would happen next. My only saving grace was that Dana attended a school on the other side of town. The best idea I had was to bury it, lay low, and hope to never see her again.

A couple of weeks later, I was invited to a party. *Me? Invited to a party?* This was a rarity (to put it lightly). I had to find a way to go.

A girl named Tracy I knew from a year prior said she'd go with me. We weren't very close, but getting a ride from her mom was my only option.

When I walked in, forty or fifty kids were already there, and the party was still growing. It was a full moon, and a flirtation with danger hung in the air. Something suddenly felt very wrong—my intuition was trying to get my attention. My insides instantly dropped in heaviness, and I was scared I was going to faint. The energy felt dark, and no sooner had I arrived than I called a ride to come pick me up. I'd have to wait 30 minutes before Matt, a guy I met at a coffee shop, would rescue me.

I uncomfortably grabbed a warm can of beer out of the back patio cooler. I slowly scanned the backyard, and when I saw Dana in the corner, all of the guidance systems in my body started firing, "DANGER!" I quickly set my beer down on a nearby patio table and decided to wait in front of the house for Matt.

As I reached my hand out for the front door knob, the door slammed open, making a loud crash against the wall. Five vicious girls burst through the door like they owned the place, and one of them shouted, *"Where the fuck is Amber?"*

Adrenaline rushed through my body. Everything seemed to slow waaaay down, and I intensely felt every beat of my heart.

(thump) In the split second I had, I said a prayer, begging to escape that moment.

(thump) A girl I didn't recognize stood in the hallway and spoke up, "She's right there," pointing at me.

(thump) My prayers weren't answered, and I knew I was fucked.

The girls swarmed me, and I was dragged backward by my clothes and hair onto the back patio. They hurled me down onto the hard dirt. I stumbled my way up, completely disoriented.

The girls surrounded me and spewed false accusations while pushing me from girl to girl in circles. The rest of the kids at the party surrounded them but didn't dare say a word. I'd never felt more alone in my life.

Dana and her best guy friend, Talon, appeared in the crowd. She snapped at the girls to shut up for a minute…long enough to tell me this is what I got for crossing her. As if rehearsed, the five girls closed in on me once more, then shoved me down onto the ground.

As I lay on the dirt, covering my face and experiencing each brutal kick to my head, back, or thigh and the screeching of their anger, my senses were hyper-aware of the fact that no one was trying to stop this from happening. Not one person. I was honestly more soulfully hurt from seeing humanity play out this way than I was from the blood and gashes I got that night.

A voice inside screamed at me to get up. I was surrounded, hurt, and alone… I just wanted to lay there and take it. And yet some other primal instinct kicked in, and my body scrambled up and ran. I sprinted through the house, slipping on the hallway rug, and out through the front door, with the girls close behind me. In the dark of night, I could barely make out the figure of Matt. My ride had come! The girls chased me around his truck, and I torpedoed in through the passenger door. Matt had no clue what was going on, but he held them back and yelled for them to back off. I just lay there in the passenger's seat of the truck, sobbing hysterically.

Matt, who was a few years older, was furious. He took me to be a kind, shy girl who wasn't dealt the easiest hand. I looked at him with feelings that he must be a guardian angel for me. He ended up exiting my life as quickly as he'd come into it, only there for a short time to protect me from the darkness that surrounded me that night.

I couldn't face my mom at home and begged Matt to take me to the coffee shop to clean up. While I was in the bathroom cleaning the rocks from my skin, I had no idea we had been followed. Kids from the party came in waves. Matt called his college friends to come back him up. It was clear…this was no longer about me. The police came to diffuse the growing contention. I was in such shock that I had no understanding of what was even happening.

The two crowds took their egos to a nearby park where it was dark and harder to draw attention. The girls huddled under a covered picnic area, and I stood further back, removed from them all. The guys swarmed each other on the grass with bats and fists. The energy and momentum were bigger than any of us. It all happened so fast…

I certainly didn't want any of this to happen! This is NOT who I was or what I wanted for my life. I wanted to be safe. I wanted to be loved. I wanted to be chosen. I wanted to tell the truth to my friend Ayla. I wanted to protect her because I wanted protection myself. And yet, my body was frozen in fear and shock. I had no control. I just watched.

Matt shouted at Talon (who stood on behalf of Dana) that it was wrong to set up a party in order to get me jumped. He demanded that Talon apologize and this would all be over.

You could hear a feather drop at that moment. I held my breath. It felt like I was going to faint.

Talon said, "I admit it was wrong…but I will *never* apologize to that bitch." He said it so calmly and with such conviction.

I let out my breath and immediately turned my back to the crowds. I could hear the sounds of fist-fighting and wrestling as I walked with heaviness to the trucks and cars in the parking lot. I climbed into the back of the first truck I saw. The bed was covered with loose dirt and gravel. I laid down in the back, and tears streamed down my cheeks.

I looked up at the stars that night, crushed, mourning my existence. I questioned, "Is this my life? Is this the way it's going to be?"

I experienced a drowning sensation, like I was slowly falling into an abyss. I was aware of just how powerless I was and how worthless I felt.

In the stars, I could sense two paths with my blurry, tear-soaked eyes. One was me continuing on the path I was going down, and it was short, ending in my early twenties. The other was a long, strong, vibrant path. It looked like a beam of light…"a light path." I didn't know what that meant, but I wanted to find out.

Talon ended up in the hospital that night. I was grounded. The bullying at school got worse.

I decided to keep my head down and my mouth shut after that. I didn't want to share my truth or use my voice. I didn't want to be seen. It just wasn't worth it. I was sick and tired of being so completely misunderstood. It was time to self-protect and hide even more than before.

Decision by decision and day by day, I'd do things differently. I stopped searching for connection, friends, and protection. Instead, I'd go in for teacher office hours and pull up my grades. I'd focus on working as a server and saving money. I dove into karate for the next two years. I disengaged from my family (nothing had changed; I just stopped trying to fit in). I graduated with Honors and received an award for being the most-improved student in my graduating class. I didn't care, I just wanted to get out of there. I'd felt so completely rejected by my classmates for so long that I just wanted a clean start after graduation, which is exactly what I did.

I stepped into a new world in college. I landed a job selling Cutco Cutlery in between classes, which woke up the giant of my entrepreneurial spirit. Throughout my twenties, I grew into a more resilient, focused, empowered woman. I was proud that I overcame my rock bottom moment early in life. I worked in the Cutco world for five years, breaking national records and getting spoiled on reward trips. *For the first time in my life, I experienced the internal freedom of feeling seen, heard, and valued. I was celebrated for my goodness. It was so refreshing that I wanted to spend my life helping others feel that way too.*

And what was really wild… Talon and Dana separately reached out to me in my mid-twenties to apologize. Both shared they were so messed up on drugs that they don't even have much memory of what had happened, but they sensed they had done something awful to me and wanted to atone. My healing journey began. I could put to rest my fear of shadows. I could begin again.

So, why did I tell you all of this?

When I was 16, I chose to use my voice and express my truth. That very action got me jumped. **As a kid who didn't know better, I unknowingly created a belief that "when I use my voice, bad things happen."** This was one of many moments that reinforced that core belief in my life. I misinterpreted the experience, and out of self-protection, I buried a big part of myself so I would never have to be hurt like that again. As a result, I spent the next two decades unknowingly in resistance to being seen and heard (especially when sharing my truth), weaving in and out of hiding, and bumping up against a glass ceiling in my company.

If I didn't get *too* well-known, I wouldn't have to be seen and heard *too much*, and rejection or negative consequences would be minimal.

The true wake-up call in my late thirties exposed all of this to me. My mentor Ken was the catalyst.

Of course, your story may be very different from mine, but undoubtedly, you experienced something in your past that created your own self-sabotaging beliefs—your resistance. And that is what we'll break down in the next chapter.

Resistance may never fully go away, but having a simple exercise (once you get the hang of it) to fall back on makes all the difference in the world (as you'll see in Chapters 3 and 12). In the pursuit of writing this book, I bumped up against many shades of my resistance to being seen and heard. You may experience something similar in your journey.

The key lies in the decision to do something about it—to move beyond it—not in a forced way, but in a more natural, conscious way that honors your past and paves the way for a deeply fulfilling future.

> "Life is not about finding yourself.
> Life is about creating yourself."
> - George Bernard Shaw

CHAPTER 3

THE COURAGE TO COURSE-CORRECT

This chapter is necessary for clearing and cultivating the land on which to build your Foundational Four Framework. It's here that we identify your resistance and shift it so you're prepared for The Work. You're about to take a GIANT step in getting *ready* to market your cause so you are responsible with its distribution and Impact.

Without first moving through the exercise presented below, you would likely do The Work, only to self-sabotage as soon as the spotlight heads in your direction. If taken seriously, this exercise will powerfully awaken you to your blind spots, and give you newfound courage to be seen and heard in much bigger ways. This is such a powerful and effective exercise that you'll find the philosophy and framework behind it repeated in future chapters.

<u>My goal is to open your awareness and offer you a space to be brutally honest with yourself so that you can make business decisions based</u>

on what is highest and best *for you*. Once you do that, you'll more naturally share your best with others, which inevitably creates a far greater Impact (as you'll see validated by research in Chapter 4).

In my process to Course-Correct, I needed to:

1. **IDENTIFY**. I listed areas in my life where I was currently experiencing resistance.
2. **EXPLORE**. I courageously looked back and wrote down specific events from my past where I had collected evidence that "if I am seen and heard, something bad will happen."
3. **EVALUATE**. I wrote out the consequences that showed up in my life as a result of that belief.
4. **SHIFT**. Finally, I examined times in my life when I was seen and heard, but instead of having a negative outcome, I experienced love and connection instead. An extremely powerful shift!

Only then did it become clear to me that I had been operating in resistance and fear based on memories from long ago. Moving forward, I had a choice to operate in courage, inspiring a more positive outcome.

It's so simple, yet I had to trust the process and go through the exercise fully a time or two before really experiencing the possibility for broader application. However, after my first time through, I felt incredibly empowered after taking responsibility. I could clearly see that there was nothing to be afraid of in being fully self-expressed—the real, authentic me! I could more confidently step into my online platform and share what was in my heart and on my mind. My engagement increased, sales closed even faster, but most of all…I finally felt free inside.

Even now, any time resistance comes up, I come back to the Courage to Course-Correct exercise. The huge benefit I couldn't have predicted when I first created this exercise is that each time I go through it (albeit from a different angle to my resistance), I've found it not only gets easier and faster but my overall resistance is being diminished in great strides.

I'm now going to guide you through the same exercise:

- I'll give you instructions up-front with writing prompts, but I encourage you to start writing freely right out of the gate. You may find it helpful to grab the "Exercises Log" document in your companion Toolkit for an additional focused writing space.
- **I invite you to look at this exercise through a lens of curiosity.**
- If you get lost or stuck or find yourself in a pocket of insecurity, I further support you with troubleshooting advice below each writing section so you have something to anchor into.
- Additionally, I'll share my own answers vulnerably so you feel connected and supported.

The work you do here will set you up for *great* success in Part 2, where we go deep with Avatar, Vision, Why, and Values exercises that will help you get and stay in Alignment.

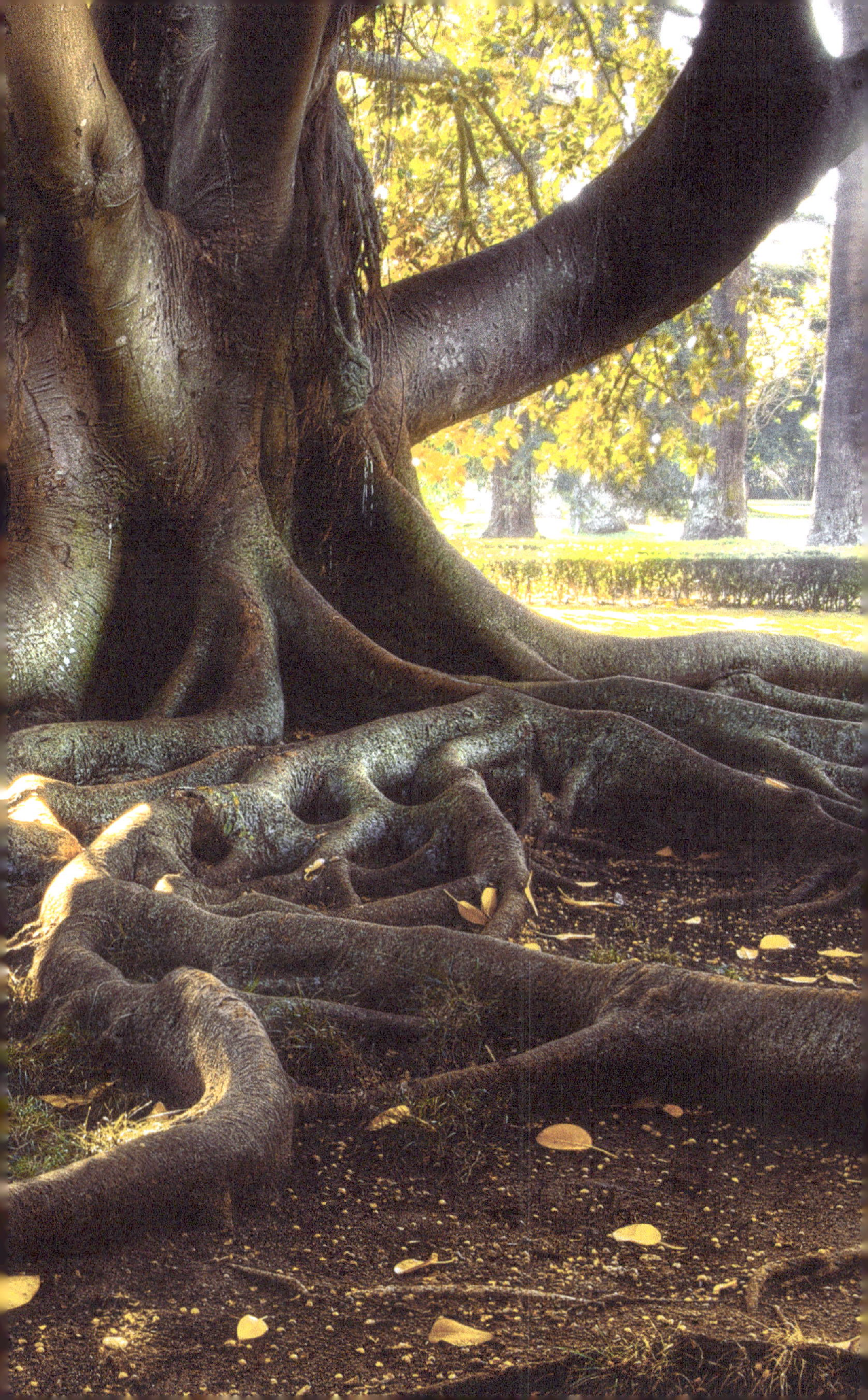

THE COURAGE TO COURSE-CORRECT EXERCISE

ENTREPRENEUR ACTION, STEP 1 [IDENTIFY]:

Get curious and list where you are currently experiencing resistance (big or small). Consider resistance tied to activities where you specifically have an increased chance of being seen or heard.

In the future, you'll examine different forms of resistance, but we start here because, in my experience, authors and professionals unanimously have some sort of resistance to being seen and heard.

Writing prompts:

- ☐ Think about where in your life you feel resistant to being seen or heard.
    - ☐ Perhaps it is before walking on stage to give a speech, or raising your hand to share something with a network, or when giving a presentation to a group.
    - ☐ It could also be when you receive an award, or get recognition after an act of service or kindness.
- ☐ Close your eyes and imagine that feeling of resistance, where you wish you could just get it over with or be anywhere else. <u>Embrace that feeling and use it to create a connection to other circumstances where you experience a similar feeling.</u>

- ☐ Perhaps you feel resistance when:
    - ☐ Getting your photo taken, being in a video shoot, or on stage.
    - ☐ Having a sales conversation, or meeting with a potential strategic partner who could amplify your cause, or being interviewed on a podcast.
    - ☐ Writing marketing, website, book, or other content that requires sharing your beliefs.
    - ☐ Fully expressing how you feel to a spouse, parent, team member, client, or perceived authority figure.
    - ☐ Wanting to wear a certain outfit, buy a certain piece of art or furniture, share a certain joke, or style your hair a certain way.
    - ☐ Seeing something you disagree with and wanting to do something about it.
- ☐ It may help to walk through your schedule in a day or even a full week to recall tiny pockets of resistance that aren't so obvious.
- ☐ Think through decisions you have a hard time making.

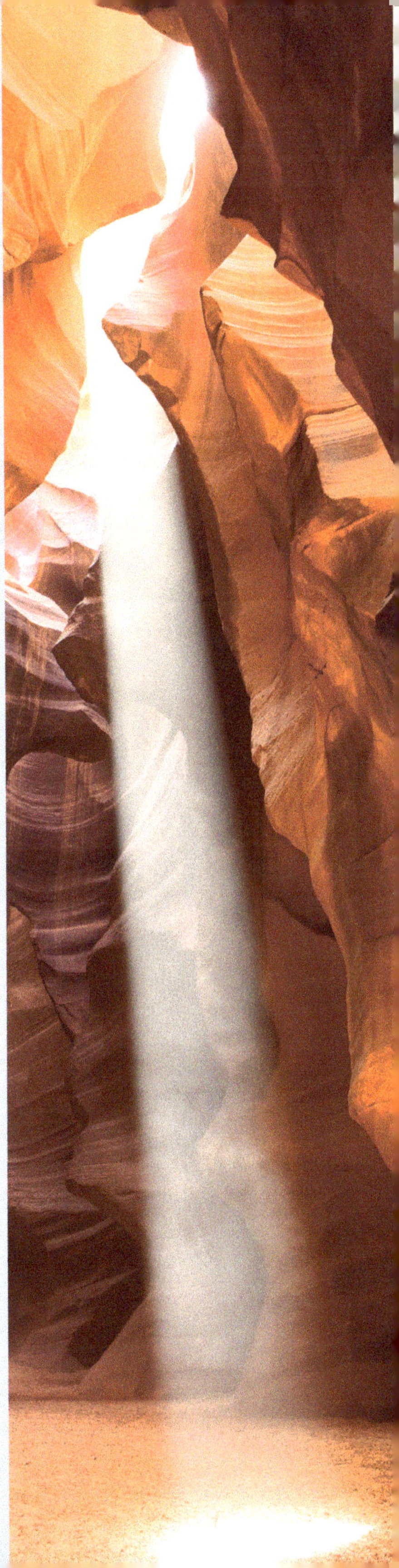

Troubleshooting:

1. This exercise may take a little time, and that's ok, t*ake the time you need*. You only need a handful of instances before you are in a good position to move on. You are not here to recount every situation where you experience resistance, just a good sampling.

2. It's important to be really honest with yourself. It may not always feel good to think about the challenging situations you are avoiding, so you may even feel resistance coming up right

now! <u>Remember, the purpose of this exercise</u> is to expose what's holding you back so you gain faster and stronger momentum toward achieving Impact (which is what you want more than you want to close the book and avoid this work).

3. It's not so much about the number of situations you can identify, it's about tapping into the feeling of resistance and exploring that emotion. Get curious about it. Follow its lead.

<u>Once you have at least 5-7 instances where you are currently experiencing resistance</u>, and believe you've really tapped into the feeling that comes up, we can now move to the second step.

Debrief: The situations you listed in Step 1 that identified your resistance offer "evidence" that a limiting core belief is presently holding you back either personally and/or professionally.

Step 2 will help you bridge a connection between your current resistance and that limiting core belief you formed in the past. Below your space to write, you'll see a Troubleshooting section where I listed my entries for your review.

ENTREPRENEUR ACTION, STEP 2 [EXPLORE]:

Courageously locate memories from your past when you collected evidence and formed a belief that "if I am seen and heard, something bad will happen." The key is to stay curious and objective, as if studying a rock formation and imagining how storms must have shaped its curvatures.

<u>Note</u>: The phrase "something bad" can encompass rejection, physical abuse, abandonment, shaming, gaslighting, aggressiveness, passive-aggressiveness, etc.—any unhealthy response.

Writing prompts:

- ☐ What happened when you tried to do the right thing and something bad happened?
- ☐ When were you edited, silenced, or ignored?
- ☐ Who stole the spotlight from you?
- ☐ What were you innocently doing when you got punished or hushed as a kid?
- ☐ Who publicly shamed or embarrassed you?
- ☐ What relationships are no longer in your life that ended badly?
- ☐ What did a sibling do to push you away or reject you?
- ☐ Who has the wrong idea about you and your beliefs?
- ☐ Who overrode your ideas and plans because they thought theirs were better?
- ☐ Which past team member, partner, or colleague misunderstood you?
- ☐ Who didn't protect you when you needed help?
- ☐ When did you feel you couldn't be fully yourself?

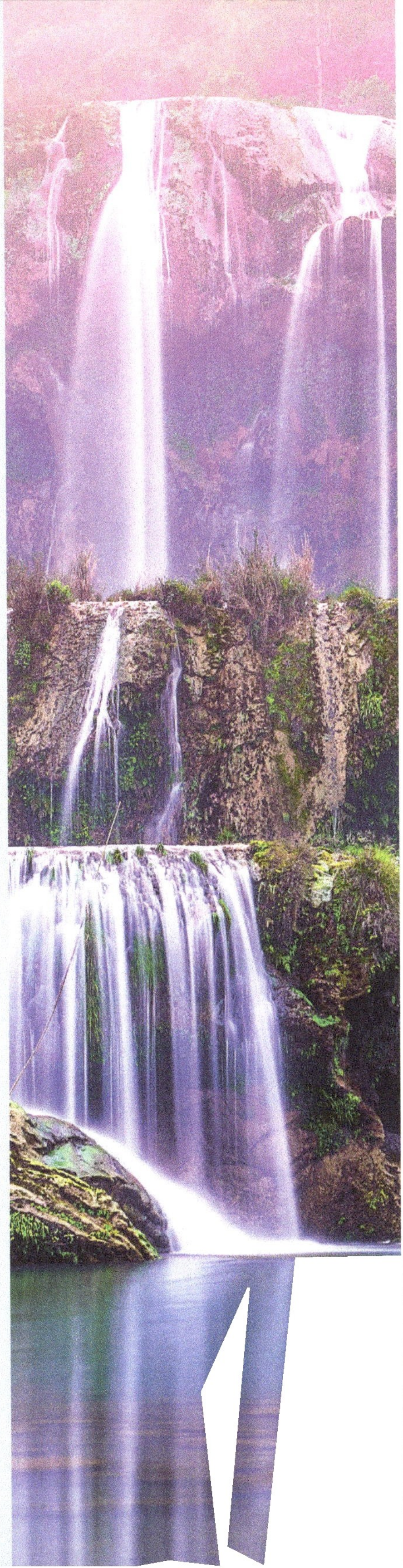

Troubleshooting:

1. The goal of this exercise is not to uproot your deepest traumas and create more fear or sadness. The goal is to note the memories that come most quickly to mind in an objective manner, as if you are studying a grasshopper's steps as it's walking around in a jar.

2. *<u>If you notice unpleasant feelings start to surface, take a strong deep breath, then slowly exhale that unwanted emotion out of your body</u>. Whatever you do, don't avoid it, shut the process down, or close the book and do something else.*

Below is a list I wrote in my journal when I first went through this exercise. In italics and parentheses, you'll see how my younger self interpreted those experiences to illustrate just how different an adult might view them, and how powerful it is to go back and address these memories and assign a new and more empowering meaning. <u>When I did this exercise, these were some things that came up for me:</u>

- My 1st birthday, family singing around my cake, my older sister had a tantrum and the singing stopped. (*When I am celebrated, people get upset.*)
- In my childhood home's hallway, I asked to play, and my sister slammed the door in my face. (*I used my voice and was rejected.*)
- 3rd grade, my best friend Emily chose Tiffany over me. (*I was in the spotlight hoping to be chosen and was rejected.*)
- 6th through 12th grade, I was bullied at school. (*I was in the spotlight and bad things happened repeatedly for years.*)
- 16, I told Ayla the secret, then got jumped by five girls. (*I used my voice and was physically harmed.*)
- My letter was edited and sent without my knowledge. (*I used my voice and was rejected.*)
- Set my first healthy boundary with a family member and got yelled at repeatedly. (*I used my voice and was threatened.*)

After making my list, I looked at the events that I had grouped together as evidence of the belief that painful things happen when I am seen or heard. **NO WONDER there was resistance** around getting on stage, recording video, publishing books, asking for help, or being fully honest in certain relationships.

Debrief: We can't be fully self-expressed and make our ultimate Impact if we keep those beliefs trapped and buried. We can't hide them away, otherwise they will continue to create resistance.

<u>Our minds and bodies are only trying to protect us from the threat of a bad result</u>. But if we don't overcome these "protection mechanisms," we won't ever know our true significance.

Recognize that *those events are in the past where they belong*, and shift your mind into celebrating that you've just uprooted some blind spots that have been slowing you down from going full throttle with marketing your cause.

In most cases, **we have no idea of the true cost of holding on to this belief** (which we were unaware of to begin with, until now), but let's explore it to get a glimpse.

> ENTREPRENEUR ACTION, STEP 3 [EVALUATE]:

Write out where your core belief ("when I am seen and heard, bad things happen" or other limiting beliefs) got you in life:

Writing prompts:

- ☐ Look at your resistance list in Step 1 to see the direct impact of that belief. You'll discover where it has been holding you back personally and professionally, as well as how it conflicts with who you want to be and how you want to show up in the world.
- ☐ Think about arguments you've had with a spouse or in a past relationship. What behaviors showed up that contributed to its challenges?
- ☐ Consider your level of presence and engagement with your children or your friend's children. Are you open or do you hold them at a distance emotionally?
- ☐ Look around your home, at your personal styling, or your office. Have you experienced resistance in decisions of self-expression?
- ☐ Consider when you are agitated, and map what triggered that reaction.

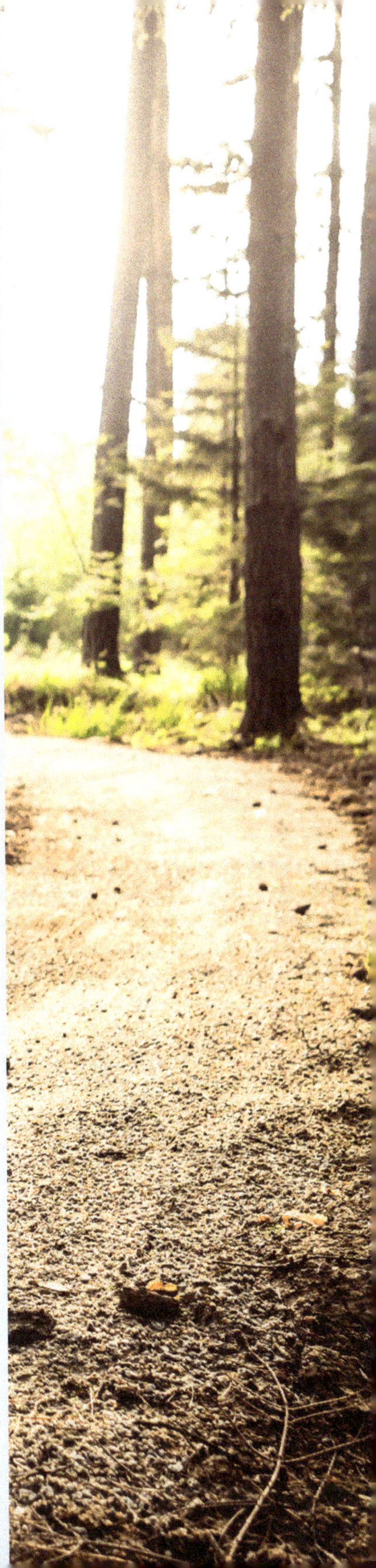

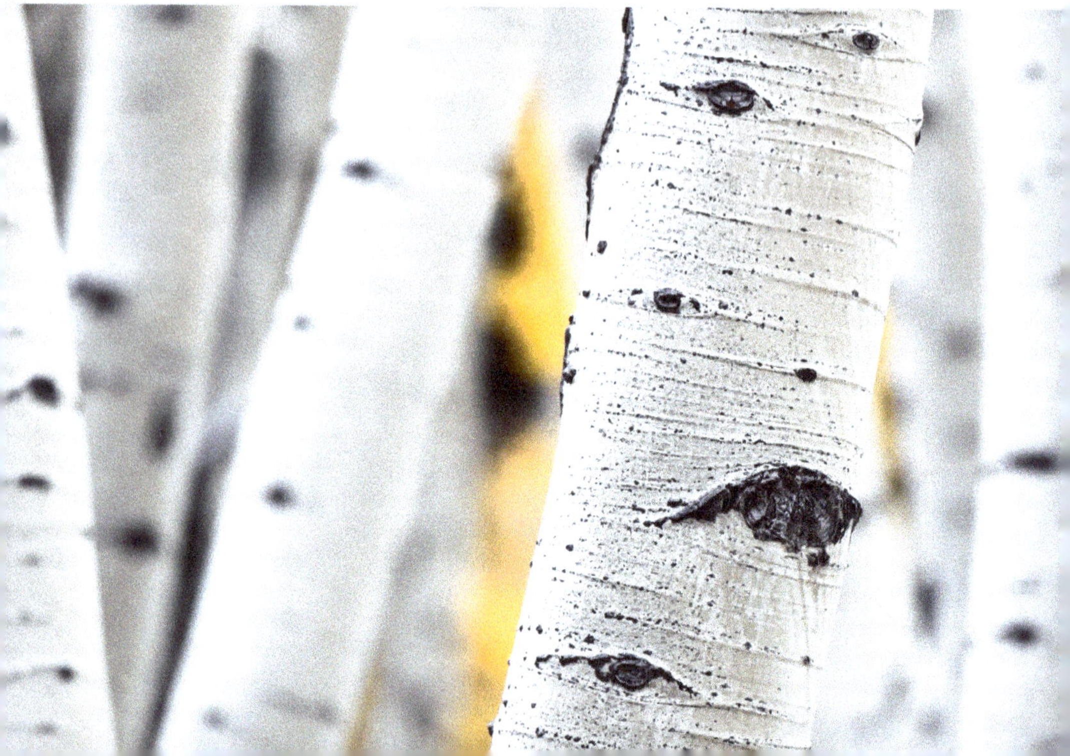

Here's where my own misinterpreted core belief got me in life:

- I was disinterested in selecting paint colors, art, or furniture for my home. I would just say, "It doesn't matter to me, you decide," proud of myself for being easygoing.
- I couldn't fully open up to or trust the people closest to me.
- I deflected praise or would quickly forget the kind things people said to me.
- I never thought to celebrate my wins. I was too busy working on the next to-do list item.
- I developed high-strung neuroticism, and an over-delivering and people-pleasing nature, then tried to keep it under wraps so even that couldn't be a source of attack. This high-achieving drive would lead to light forms of escapism to give my nervous system a break.
- I struggled with being a strong advocate for others—taking a stand wasn't a quick and obvious decision.
- I deeply internalized a lot of what I experienced in life, telling myself it was best to keep those feelings behind closed doors.

Debrief: Let's unpack what may have just come up for you in what I call the "messy middle." You are doing some deep work here... exploring memories you misinterpreted, which formed a belief, initiated subconscious decision-making, influenced your behaviors, and resulted in life experiences that were less than desirable. And, if you don't continue the process, that will keep happening in a loop.

I was shocked by the writing that came out of me during this part of the exercise. I flashed back to memories of arguments with loved ones, times when I felt shame for not speaking up, regret for not being a stronger advocate for others, and worst of all...*I saw how that core belief ultimately created a life experience where I was not valued by MYSELF. (Ouch.)*

This momentum was all the motivation I needed to innovate a shift so I wasn't stuck in these old, tired patterns.

To set up the fourth and final step in this exercise:

- In Step 1, you listed the areas of your life where you are currently experiencing resistance. We did that to help you recognize the *emotion* of resistance.

- Then in Step 2, you examined times in your life when you collected the evidence that formed a belief that "when I was seen and heard, something bad happened." You connected the *emotion* in Step 1 to those memories.

- Similarly, you'll want to cultivate an emotion here to support the new belief you form in Step 4 below. Instead of an emotion of resistance, I want you to experience emotions of success, accomplishment, love, and especially pride. Start by thinking of times you felt highly proud of yourself.

| ENTREPRENEUR ACTION, STEP 4 [SHIFT]: |

Examine times in your life when you were seen and heard, but instead of having a negative outcome, <u>you experienced love and acceptance</u>. You are now shifting into collecting evidence that the **opposite** of that once-held belief is true. This will offer you a new, empowering belief to *replace* the old, limiting belief.

Writing prompts:

- ☐ Think of the times when you naturally acted in service or kindness to someone in need.
- ☐ Remember a time you shared something special or vulnerable on social media or in your email marketing and got a comment back thanking you.
- ☐ Think of a time recently when you shared your honest, good-hearted thoughts, assessment, feelings, or views on a team member's performance, a child's challenging behavior, or response to pain caused by a loved one, and your honesty was received (not rejected) and even appreciated.
- ☐ Recall a time when you honestly shared your needs or set a healthy boundary, and regardless of how it was received, it carried a positive charge because you were true to you. (*This points to self-love.*)
- ☐ Remember times when you walked off stage, closed a virtual meeting room, or finished recording video and felt a high sense of accomplishment for leaving it all on the line.
- ☐ Consider conversations you've had with a mentor, authority figure, therapist, or other professional and how they responded to your honest thoughts and feelings.
- ☐ Think of a time when you paused your schedule to help a friend in need and how they reacted to your choice.

- ☐ Look at areas of your life where you show up in service, such as volunteering at church or a school, and consider how you are viewed and appreciated.
- ☐ Consider any proof of self-love present in your home (equivalent to my purple wall, twinkle lights, choice in artwork, etc.). Reflect on how you are being self-expressed in your home, on your body, at work, etc.

Troubleshooting:

1. If you get stuck, ask a team member, spouse, or friend to help you remember times of accomplishment and joy.
2. Don't judge the number of experiences you come up with. Keep ruminating on the exercise and see what comes up for you tomorrow after a good night's sleep if need be.

Debrief: When beliefs are deeply explored, they can reveal contradictions.

For example, sometimes, I step out in courage and have a negative outcome. Other times, I step out in courage and have a positive outcome.

That's because we formed these beliefs as little kids and haven't taken the time to explore and redefine them as adults.

(Therefore, my previous mode of operation was to be careful and try to discern when it was safe to step out and when it wasn't. I'd operate in contradiction and choose to play small, but at least I'd (maybe) get hurt a little less.) Allow the findings in Step 4 to inspire and refocus you.

You now have evidence that there were times when you showed up in kindness, honoring your voice, with the courage to be seen, and the sky didn't fall!

Yes, really unfortunate things happened to us as we aged. We can consciously examine those memories and see the gift in them, but the body keeps score and holds on to the hurt in an attempt to better protect us from future threats.

That's why we have to see and accept our personal responsibility to expose our blind spots, make different behavior choices, choose self-trust and self-love, choose to stay open and in service, and consciously *receive* the recognition and love that comes our way.

It's time to collect more of the right kind of evidence that being seen and heard is a good thing because it sure is necessary to make Infinite Impact.

After I was done with all four Steps in the exercise, I reflected back. The biggest sting to me was my journaling in Step 3, where I saw the impact of my misinterpreted, limiting belief. No, it wasn't fun or awesome to take responsibility for how I was behaving toward others, but **a big "aha"** for me in this process was seeing that my new behavior choices shifted the way I felt about *myself*. I started to experience what other people promoted as self-love. To me, that looked like:

- Choosing to paint my office wall purple because that honored my true choice, which sparked a passion to paint more walls, redecorate, and add more twinkle lights. That honoring is self-love.
- Choosing to be open and trusting in relationships, which meant I was trusting myself to handle that option. That is another expression of self-love.
- Choosing to receive recognition and trusting it was safe to be seen and heard. That is self-love as well.

I learned that when I believed in self-trust and self-love, I tapped into a superpower that gave me an endless source of courage to be fully self-expressed in the marketing of my cause. When *I* was my best, I expressed my best, and I created connections with others faster and more easily than ever before. As I said, my business engagement increased, sales closed even faster, but most of all…I finally felt free inside.

The Courage to Course-Correct isn't a checklist item. It's something we practice for the rest of our lives. It's an opportunity to go deep, learn more and more about ourselves, and then express our findings with others to inspire them to continue their practice too. This was really crucial prep work before heading into *Part 2: The Work.*

You'll be referring back to this exercise throughout the book, so commit the following sequence to memory so you can Course-Correct in the future any time resistance hits:

1. **IDENTIFY.** Be aware of your resistance and examine what it feels like.
2. **EXPLORE.** Consider times in your past when you've had that feeling and the limiting belief that was formed as a result.
3. **EVALUATE.** Consider the cost of continuing to let resistance hold you back from being fully self-expressed.
4. **SHIFT.** Remember you've faced your fears and experienced a good outcome plenty of times. Choose to shift into courage, be open to the possibility of a great outcome, and focus on Impact.

Each chapter has some lighter, but related, exercises and lots of opportunities for your team to do the heavy lifting afterward.

You showed immense Courage to Course-Correct and have now tapped into the source (self-trust and self-love) to keep gaining more and more courage as you experience new levels of success in the marketplace. This work gave you more readiness for advocacy, and it's an honor to have been a part of it.

"The better you know yourself,
the better your relationship with
the rest of the world."
- Toni Collette

I'm doing the work!

Part of my Core Values is that we are better together. I want to meaningfully connect with each person who interacts with my work. Please email me at amber@infiniteimpactbook.com with the subject line: "I'M DOING THE WORK" as a proclamation that we're in this together now and there's no turning back. I'll reply, and we can celebrate your choice.

CHAPTER 4
ALIGNMENT

Your business is like the game of Jenga. If one piece is out of Alignment, it threatens the stability of the entire structure. (You'll learn a lot more about this in Chapter 10.) When I was out of Alignment, I ended up hiring many of the wrong people (people who were out of Alignment with my Foundational Four). I fast-tracked some projects and delayed others, not anchoring them into my Why. I was all over the place in my mind, and my body was stiff and aching from the stress of relentlessly trying to uncover my blind spots.

My internal struggle regrettably presented as being guarded and short with loved ones. I remember wishing for life's carousel ride to pause just long enough for me to catch my breath and reorient—but instead, time just kept flying by, and customer demands continued to grow.

Year after year, I was making *great strides on paper*, while quietly enduring an excruciating repair period of deconstructing what I had built, re-Aligning the company, and forging ahead in a more congruent way. That was my experience, but being out of Alignment can show up in many different forms.

SIGNS YOU MIGHT BE OUT OF ALIGNMENT

Most prospects come to me saying things like, "I don't like social media. I don't want to be an Influencer. I don't know who to trust to do it for me. I feel stuck." **These individuals are NOT yet ready to make the Impact they crave.**

Further, in the early stages of working together, most of my clients wrestle with me about their:

- Monetization model (thinking they should build automated courses for the masses instead of higher-value offers that cultivate meaningful connection),
- Pricing (devaluing themselves, mistakenly charging way too little for the immense value they bring to the table because they subconsciously feel unworthy), and
- Customer journey (a confusing sales process leaving prospects feeling unsure, too many entry points, multiple funnels with tripwires, and unnecessarily long nurture sequences).

The **incongruence** these authors and professionals experience in their marketing and sales models is rampant, leading to self-sabotaging behavior and/or crushing results.

And hey, if this is hitting a little close to home, don't beat yourself up. You don't know what you don't know, and the internet is FULL of smoke and mirrors. Self-proclaimed gurus make offers based on something that worked for them without much consideration for how different each business owner is. It's easy to follow them and adopt "should" thinking. (This looks like, "I should make a course" or "I should build a large following.")

I'm here to set the record straight by telling you the only thing you should be doing is making business decisions from a clear, Aligned place. We'll accomplish this starting in the next chapter. Then get a thoughtful, customized business strategy (see Chapter 11) because generic cookie-cutter strategies are unlikely to work successfully for you.

It's VERY RARE to find a strategist who both understands and encourages your uniqueness—someone who can work with you to customize a marketing, sales, and growth plan that is congruent with and a natural self-expression of your Foundational Four. By getting into Alignment myself, I am now able to support my clients in leading from an Aligned place too.

WHY IS NOW THE MOST IMPORTANT TIME TO GET AND STAY IN ALIGNMENT?

(Reader Note: Read this section very carefully, please.)

Putting it plainly, being in Alignment will help you market your cause authentically, and authentic content will win consumer attention moving forward.

We live in an era when misinformation and artificially created content are on the rise. Unsuspecting homeowners are receiving phone calls from hackers pretending to be the President of The United States or other authority figures. Videos stream in our social media feed *look* like a recording of a human, only to find out it was fully computer-generated. We are now becoming more aware of gaslighting and manipulation due to the rise of individuals experiencing serious mental health challenges.

This rise of misinformation and manipulation will require us to do two things differently:

1. As a Consumer: Drastically improve our individual, internal process for discernment so we know who and what to trust
2. As an Entrepreneur: Understand the precious value of our unique, authentic voice and refuse to let it be diminished.

Breaking down the consumer experience:

Can you imagine a world where we trust even less than we do now? I find myself in a frenzy at times, wondering what else I can do to help humanity shift so that my son has genuine experiences of meaningful connection with others. I shudder to think what will happen as our current state accelerates exponentially.

As far as I can tell, there's one way forward for now, and that is to prioritize cultivating a stronger relationship with your own intuition—your gut instinct—*and this book will help you do just that.* Your intuition is that internal voice that tells you you've taken a wrong turn while driving, for example. It's an immediate knowing of something without mental or emotional reasoning or evidence. I now believe more than ever that our individual intuition is our resource for ultimate truth.

By trusting the answers and guidance you get internally, you'll be protected in confusing moments, and innately know who and what to trust. (I've personally experienced this more times than I can count.) The invitation is to exercise and build the muscle of—build trust in—our intuition so that the voice gets louder and louder. The more we listen to and act based on what that voice tells us, the more we cultivate self-trust.

Breaking down the entrepreneur experience:

> *By trusting your ideas and unique voice, and making the courageous choice to be fully self-expressed, you will more naturally attract qualified buyers and scale your Impact.*

In the past two decades, I've experienced this enough in my own marketing and sales to know it to be true. Thankfully, more and more research also points to the immense powers of communicating authentically.

The Scale of Positive and Negative Experience (SPANE) is a research project that measured the emotions of more than 25,000 participants. By comparing how strongly individuals felt closely related emotions (such as joyful vs. happy), the research indicated that humans feel **authenticity** even more strongly than love. Authenticity points to being true, honest, genuine, and pure.

Humans can most strongly resonate and connect when another is communicating openly with pure, honest conviction. This is the prize of being in Alignment with your Avatar, Vision, Why, and Values.

When you create helpful content with authenticity (using your natural instincts—intuition), you will *naturally* connect with your audience better than if you hide or hold back.

Bring all of yourself to market, instead of a compartmentalized piece of you.

Are you seeing how a business owner's mass production of artificial content could become problematic? Hundreds of millions of social posts were being published DAILY *before* AI could produce a year's worth of content instantaneously. This sheer volume of objective (not emotional) content is flooding all communication channels. Books are being written by AI in 15 minutes and launched on Amazon in another 30 (which is why I added the "human-made" sticker to my cover—this book took me hundreds of hours to write, and I'm damn proud of that).

Let me be very clear that I am grateful for AI! I use it to help me think. I'm just unwilling to have it replace the uniqueness and power of my true voice.

Ghostwriters and AI can speed up content production, *but they cannot communicate authentically on your behalf.* Therefore, you can opt to get help in those ways, but it will come at a cost to your conversion and Impact.

Choosing to be authentic in the world is the fullest expression of you. And that's my plea to you—==be fully self-expressed moving forward.== Not hiding, not hiring someone else to write for you…but rather, trusting your own voice and style.

A good friend, Mark B. Murphy, always says, "I'm not afraid of being different. I'm afraid of being the same as everyone else." As a critical thinker and wealth strategist for entrepreneurs, Mark is a huge advocate for finding what differentiates you.

And guess what? Sharing content authentically is your most natural and most powerful differentiator. Add in some seriously effective strategies and a proven approach to optimizing your marketing, sales, and operations…and you will have a tremendous competitive advantage!

When your Avatar, Vision, Why, and Values are in Alignment, and you express your cause naturally, the marketplace will literally FEEL your congruence and be attracted into your orbit for anything you can offer them.

Infinite Impact is inevitable.

We were designed to connect in tribes. You are not supposed to be all things to all people. When you communicate authentically, you will attract like-minded people, and repel those who aren't a fit. How freeing is that!

However, when you hide or diminish the power of your voice by having someone or something else write on your behalf, you'll get the bad eggs with the good ones, making for a more challenging experience for everyone.

Now might be a good time to go back and peek at your answers from Chapter 1's Congruence Assessment. You will be more likely to identify the cost of being out of Alignment. And, if you can imagine scoring 5's on each statement, you can then imagine how freeing and exciting it can be to operate in Alignment. It's really remarkable!

SOME OF WHAT YOU ARE LIKELY TO EXPERIENCE WHEN YOU OPERATE IN ALIGNMENT

PERSONALLY

- Things become easier (you stop pushing boulders up a hill) and there is less internal pull to people-please or conform to someone else's way of doing things.
- You experience more joy and connection with a small group (such as family or team) as well as larger communities (your audience, the global community).
- You find the courage to use your voice, be seen in the world, and work in collaboration with others.
- There is less conflict and division between work and personal priorities, resulting in a more "whole life" integrated experience.
- Strong momentum is created and you achieve legacy and Impact sooner while enjoying full self-actualization. This brings more personal freedom and renewed energy and focus at a younger age when you have more energy to play!
- It sets a very powerful model/example for children and the community at large.

PROFESSIONALLY

- Alignment provides the decision-making tools you need to effectively set healthy boundaries and encourage a high level of individual accountability throughout your organization.
- There is less team and customer conflict and increased retention.

- Better outcomes are achieved with your team by hiring the right people sooner.
- Qualified buyers are attracted faster because they resonate with your authenticity, leading to higher conversion in the sales process.
- Alignment creates a quality overall brand experience that grows word-of-mouth (the most powerful form of advertising) for free!
- You will be able to more quickly and effortlessly create and distribute engaging content.
- In my experience, Alignment leads to a great reputation and long-standing business success (regardless of formal education).

You can't skip The Work of getting and staying in Alignment and expect your marketing, sales, and operations strategies to bring you high degrees of success. Without that piece in place, you will experience serious consequences as you grow. Worse, you won't be sure of what the problem is. As stated at the beginning of this chapter, it can result in wrong hires, unsuccessful product launches, frustrating stagnation with your social media channels, and so much more. It is mentally and physically exhausting to find the needle in the haystack.

Put simply, in the next Part of this book, we'll do The Work to get you in Alignment. Then in Part 3, we'll apply that knowledge to optimize your marketing, sales, and operations. You'll need some customized strategies to ensure you're moving ahead in congruence, but that's the easy part and our Books & Business community is here to fully support you with that. In the meantime, I will share my company's strategies with you in Chapters 10 and 11. The only other thing to keep on your radar as you move forward into making your Impact is when the pesky resistance surfaces. But remember, you now have a solution using the exercise in Chapter 3.

You are now well-positioned to move forward on this journey toward achieving congruence!

> "Authenticity is the daily practice of letting go of who we think we're supposed to be and embracing who we are."
> - Brené Brown

PART TWO
―――

THE WORK

CHAPTER 5

AVATAR

It was 2:00 pm on a Tuesday in 2010, and a guy named Larry called me for our scheduled hour-long sales call. He needed a new website and wanted to know my rates.

My last four sales calls hadn't been successful. Prospects kept saying they'd get back to me, and I was crushed. More than that, I really needed to onboard a new client to keep the cash flowing in my business. My mortgage payment was due, and bills were piling up. I was stressed, and the stakes were high.

My call with Larry started like any other sales call. I used the first few minutes to "build rapport," as I learned in my Cutco sales training years prior. I asked him questions, trying to find something I could build off of to create a meaningful connection.

Five minutes into the call, I'm hopeful. He starts to tell me what he's looking for in a website.

Ten minutes into the call, that familiar feeling of dread sets in. I could already tell Larry was not the type of client I ultimately wanted to work with. He distributed paper products to restaurants. He was not an author, speaker, or coach. He was not dedicated to making the world a better place. He was just trying to sell napkins and toilet paper to local restaurant chains.

I remained open and somewhat optimistic. I knew I'd do a great job for him even if the project itself didn't light me up.

Twenty-five minutes into the call he asked, *"So Amber, what's the process if you build my website?"* I went step-by-step through the process like I always did on sales calls.

Then, he asked me the question that always made me nervous, *"And what's it gonna cost me?"* I always felt this sinking feeling because I didn't know if a prospect would think my rates were high or fair, and I'd already spent a lot of time on the call just to get to this point. It was always an unpredictable outcome.

I told him about my packages and rates as confidently as I could. I knew it was over when he hesitated and told me he'd get back to me. I ended the call as professionally and kindly as I could, trying to mask the deep frustration I felt.

After ending another hour-long sales call with nothing gained for either myself or the prospect, I put my face in my hands and thought, "There *has* to be a better way!"

In the early stages of business, it's so common to ignore our intuition—the voice that tells us a prospect isn't right for us, or that trying to "help everyone" may not be effective. We just want the sale, and we'll figure out the rest *later*. (Sound familiar?)

With decades of experience now behind me, I can clearly and confidently tell you that:

Trying to help everyone is NOT the way toward success and personal fulfillment.

Instead, it usually leads to customer conflict, internal frustrations, refunds, confusion, team exits, and financial waste. If you want to avoid that laundry list of pain, pay close attention to this first pillar of the Foundational Four Framework: Avatar.

Larry ended up being one of the most instrumental people in my career. This one-hour call helped me innovate some key business practices, which I then shared with thousands of others across the world.

Larry helped me to:

1. Innovate a truly sexy customer journey that has worked extremely well for more than a decade. (I will share this in greater detail with you in Chapter 10.) It was the solution to the thought, "There has to be a better way!"

2. Lean into being honest with myself about who I wanted to work with most. From there, I grew my courage—based on the exercise below—to niche down and release the possibility of helping people outside of my new boundaries.

It was incredible for me to get so clear about who I wanted to work with—and really spend life with—the most…

Her name is Heather, and I first imagined her when I was 26 years old.

And even though presently the majority of my clients are men, they all embody the values and experiences of Heather to one degree or another.

- Heather is a 45-year-old mom who adores her two children, Matt and Haley.

- She and her husband met after college at a friend's birthday party. Their Values are rooted in honesty, loyalty, integrity, and enjoyment.
- On the weekends, their family regularly attends church. They go camping in the summertime and ski in the winter.
- Heather transitioned from her last job to pursue part-time entrepreneurship. Her husband was the breadwinner, and her kids were in middle school at the time.
- She has a huge passion for giving back and helping lift others up through her inspiring cause rooted in self-care. She had "lost herself" in the process of raising her children, but now finds connection through yoga, eating better, and supporting other women who feel lost.
- Heather wakes up early in the morning and immediately pumps herself up for the day, generating as much energy and enthusiasm as she can, knowing she's got to be productive and make the most out of her time away from the kids.
- Time tends to slip away from her as she checks social media and surfs the web. Most days, she finds herself in a rush to manage chores and errands.
- She grabs a Starbucks coffee after lunch and pumps herself up again to make progress in the afternoon.
- She does some work on her business with talk shows playing in the background. She spends 45 minutes writing a powerful and deep blog post about overcoming obstacles, but then gets frustrated about making the formatting look good and never posts it.
- By 2:00 pm, she begins to feel the pressure of her work hours coming to an end. Her kids come home from school, and the busyness of motherhood becomes her reality again.

- Heather races to the store in her SUV and listens to country music as she drives. At the store, she grabs chicken, broccoli, and a pasta side. In the checkout, she peruses the latest People magazine and begins to feel defeated about her day for not getting more done.
- Knowing she must keep up her self-esteem for her family, she pushes her frustration (that she's not making fast enough progress) aside.
- After dinner, dishes, and laundry, Heather's day is all but over. She musters up the little energy she has left to crawl into bed, kiss her husband, chat a little, and then pick up the self-help book on her nightstand, hoping for a little pick-me-up before bed.
- Tired, defeated, and lonely, she tells herself tomorrow will be better and drifts off to sleep.
- Around 2:30 am, she wakes to use the restroom—awake just long enough for her mind to start obsessing about her worries. Panicked thoughts of self-lack, financial fear, not making enough progress, loneliness, and doubt...all race through her mind as she struggles to get her thoughts to stop.
- She turns to her snoring husband, sighs, and wonders how long he will support this "hobby" of hers, and how much longer she has before he starts to resent her for using a little of their savings for her business.
- A small voice inside reassures her that she CAN reach her Vision, she can Impact others, she can feel financial independence, she can travel and love and build community...she just needs more time.
- For now, she'll get the last couple of hours of sleep she can and hopes things will turn out better tomorrow. She has faith.

In traditional Avatar exercises, you will experience an output sounding something like:

"I want to work with people who are between 35-65 years old, have some college experience, have an average of 2.5 children, and work as an employee at a large company."

You have to admit that marketing to a 65-year-old man nearing retirement who has four kids is vastly different from marketing to a 35-year-old woman who has one kid and is still building momentum in her career.

That's why I needed a more advanced exercise, and I thank an early mentor, Eric Graham, for giving me such a powerful gift in this exercise early in my career.

When you create a short marketing video, or write a piece of content, with good-hearted intent to help such a large range of individuals… your natural language and resonance fall flat because you are too diluted—too general—in your delivery, which has a drastic impact on your results. You are trying to be all things to all people.

The results come out looking like the same overused marketing messages we are all tired of seeing. **They lack depth and richness.**

This is a common blind spot and a big reason why so many authors and professionals are grouchy about their lack of results with marketing.

Deep and thoughtful specificity in your content is catnip for your marketing.

And that is something AI can't produce. You find the language by doing The Work.

My connection with Heather is so intimate and real that when I go to record a video, I imagine Heather *craving* someone to see her and value her. I imagine her at her computer, feeling insecure that her business looks more like a hobby, longing for a following that meaningfully engages with her content. She knows there's something there, but doesn't have the public validation yet to the degree she believes everyone else does. She thinks she's putting it all on the line, and yet she's also self-sabotaging, hiding, and fumbling her way through a little bit.

When I record a video for Heather, my emotions and Why are activated. Therefore, I can get much more specific in my delivery. I can get much more intimate because I "see" her.

<u>I know Heather so well by now that I can visualize exactly what she is thinking and feeling, moment by moment, as she goes through her daily life.</u>

I know when she's self-loathing, when she's ready for someone to hold her firmly accountable, and when she's riding high on top of the world. I can intuit her greatest hopes and deepest insecurities and fears. In my marketing, I put on my coach hat and give her what she needs consistently, week in and week out because *she deserves that from me.*

When you get that specific in your marketing, no matter what your cause is, your words become sticky. They connect and linger in the viewer's mind and heart.

As a side note, you'll recall most prospects come to me saying things like, "I don't like social media. I don't want to be an Influencer. I feel stuck." Those same individuals tell me they have no problem talking 1:1 with people.

By doing The Work and marketing specifically to your Avatar, it will feel like you're having an ongoing 1:1 conversation with that person. You'll experience the joy, momentum, and confidence of making a real Impact. The dread that weighed on you before will die off and be replaced by a true enjoyment for marketing. This is quite different from what most marketing experts teach these days. When you experience the outcome, you will wish you'd heard this sooner.

Once you fully adopt everything I'm teaching you in this book, you'll begin having sales calls with ideal, qualified prospects. And just like I often hear on my calls, you'll hear, "I'm so happy to be here! I watched so many of your videos, and I feel like you were talking directly to me. I'm ready to move forward right away." I often experience those words within minutes of meeting someone new because I'm Aligned. And it means so, so much to me because that expression means I'm achieving my Vision.

My Vision is to help individuals feel seen, heard, and valued (which then satisfies my Why). Heather (my Avatar) and I share a key set of Values. And since I had the Courage to Course-Correct, I can approach my marketing to her by being specific and open, which creates a meaningful connection so she feels safe to engage me as her strategist, coach, and friend. I will experience my Impact through her growth and her own Impact.

> Do you see The Work we are doing here starting to come together?

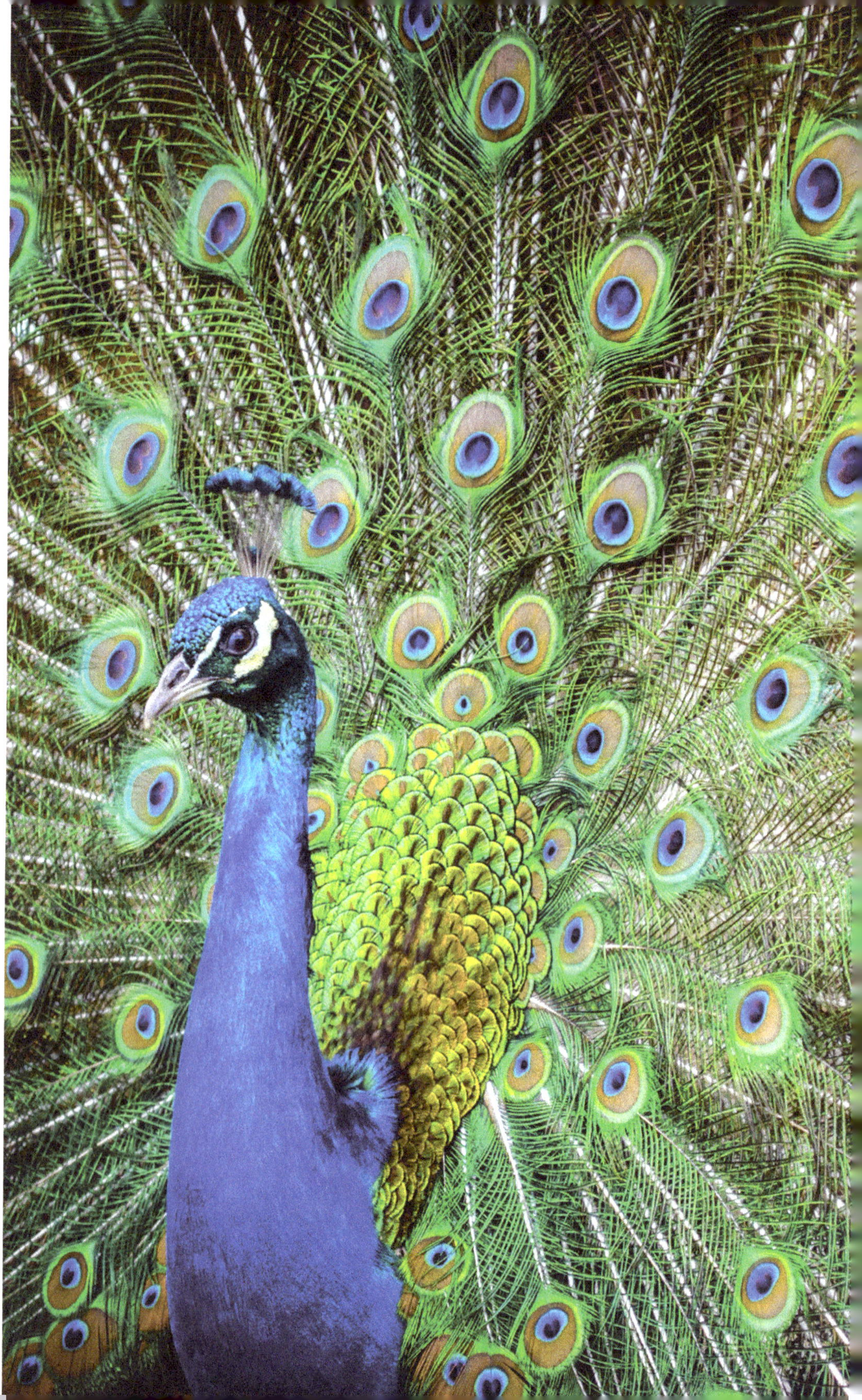

AVATAR EXERCISE

If you're ready to grow your engagement and overall sales conversion with qualified prospects, let's dig in and complete the final exercise to get and stay in Alignment.

ENTREPRENEUR ACTION, STEP 1:

Write out a specific profile and day in the life of your ideal customer.

Writing prompts:

- ☐ What is your person's gender?
- ☐ What is their exact age? (NOT a range)
- ☐ Do they have any children? If yes, how many and what are their specific ages?
- ☐ Are they single, married, divorced, widowed, separated, on a second marriage, etc.?
- ☐ Does this person have tons of friends or 1-2 close friends?
- ☐ Are they well-liked by everybody but feel lonely?
- ☐ How do they feel about their social relationships?
- ☐ What boundaries do they hold with the people in their lives?
- ☐ Does anyone "truly" know who they are?
- ☐ How do they sleep at night?
- ☐ What do they think about while falling asleep? What keeps them up at night?
- ☐ What gets them excited to wake up in the morning?
- ☐ How do they take care of themselves physically? Or how do they hide?

- [ ] How do they take care of themselves mentally? Or how do they escape?
- [ ] What do they worry about? What makes them anxious? What overwhelms them?
- [ ] What are their vices?
- [ ] What are their unmet needs?
- [ ] What are their fears?
- [ ] What are their talents?
- [ ] Where do they meet resistance?
- [ ] Do they know their goals?
- [ ] Do they know themselves?
- [ ] What do they think about what you teach?
- [ ] What are their guilty pleasures?
- [ ] What do they feel but are afraid to say?
- [ ] Are they an employee? Do they love their job, or are they quietly job hunting? What is the relationship like with their co-workers and boss? How long have they been employed at this company?
- [ ] Are they an entrepreneur? What's the size of their team? What's their revenue? Can someone at this economic stage afford your top services? Is this person at the stage of doing it all in their business (sales, fulfillment, etc.), or are they better at delegating? Have they created a process for training, culture, values, etc.?
- [ ] Are they burnt out?
- [ ] Do they vacation?
- [ ] How many hours a week do they work?

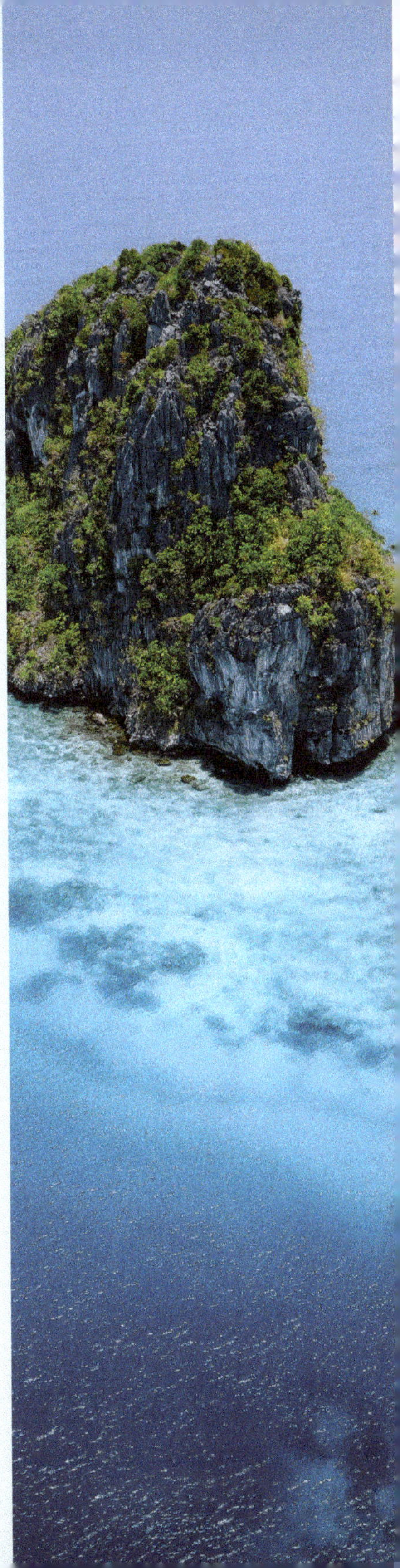

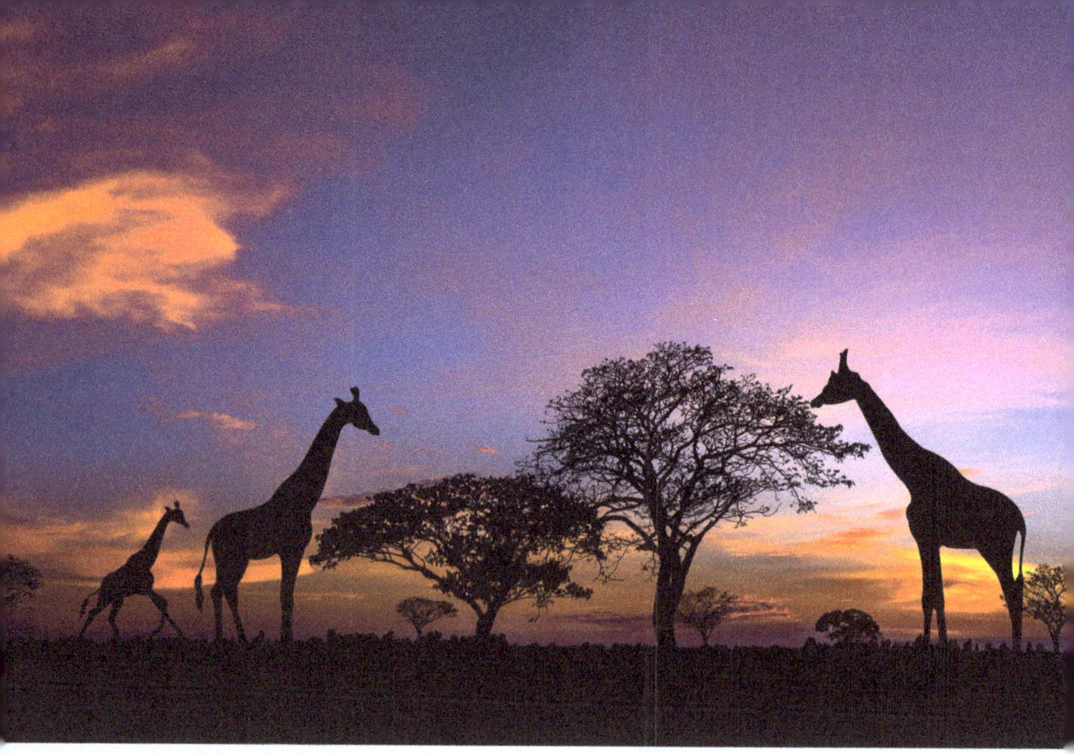

Troubleshooting:

1. It may help you to read my Avatar profile for additional prompts. You do not need to follow my format. Allow the storyteller in you to come out and play here.

2. This exercise requires tapping into your imagination (which may be rusty for some) and is a highly intuitive process. Do NOT edit yourself, or make judgments about what comes out, or try to outsmart the process. (Trust me, I've seen it all on coaching calls.)

3. You will see similarities between your life and that of your Avatar. That is normal and good. You, of course, want to feel a deep connection with the people you choose to spend so much of your life with.

4. It may help to consider past clients you loved working with, colleagues you admire, and aspects of yourself that make you feel proud.

5. Try to form a clear picture in your mind of what this person looks like. Some people go to Google Images and search for a photo of a random stranger resembling their Avatar.

ENTREPRENEUR ACTION, STEP 2:

Give your Avatar a first name.

Troubleshooting:

1. This is a really critical step, so please take it seriously. What name comes to you naturally?

2. Try to avoid this being the name of a spouse, family member, significant past client, or friend. The reason is that if that person ever created an impression with you that shifted your association with your Avatar, it could muddy your marketing moving forward.

TEAM ACTION LIST:

1. Type out a formal profile description and "day in the life" of your Avatar, and include it in your workbook.
2. Make sure EVERY team member, mentor, and/or vendor fully understands your Avatar's needs moving forward.
3. Explore ways to cultivate your own relationship and connection with this person. Exercise that muscle until you can anticipate the needs of your Avatar. This will help you offer relevant ideas and solutions for the business moving forward.

In working with *so many* authors and professionals through this exercise, some common FAQs have surfaced:

Q. Does the Avatar ever change as your company grows?

> A. Not in my experience. However, your Avatar will undergo different stages of growth as you grow and expand your offerings.
>
> For example, in the early years of NGNG, Heather was in the startup phase of her business. She did a lot of work herself, she was a solopreneur with no team, she was much more insecure, she had very little starting budget to hire outside help from vendors, and she experienced a lot of trial-and-error with her messaging, positioning, and initial offers.
>
> As my career developed and I raised my rates and enhanced my offers, I started to market to Heather at a stage when she had grown her business effectively to six figures annually. She felt more confident in her day-to-day life. She was aware that blind spots existed, she just didn't know what they were or how to move beyond them. She was open to investing a little more money into higher-level mentorship, web design, or marketing support. She had a tiny team and made the decision to step up even more and see what she could build with the solid business she had created.
>
> And then, as I continued to evolve personally and professionally, I envisioned Heather later in her career as she was just past the seven-figure mark in her company. She had a lot more responsibility, she was more well-known in her industry, a lot of cash was flowing through her company, and she was starting to save. In fact, she switched roles with her husband and was

proud to have become the primary breadwinner at home. She felt more pain stemming from those blind spots, so she hired high-tier mentors and consultants to actualize her potential even faster than she had done previously.

And so on and so forth.

In reviewing my current business model, I have tons of high-value, free content online to serve Stage 1 Heather.

For Stage 2 Heather, I run transformational in-person events and put my best work into digital programs that teams can utilize to learn and implement my strategies in-house, which saves Heather money to reinvest in her company's growth.

Stage 3 Heather has the budget and knows the value of hiring me to be "All In" for the growth marathon she's on. These clients pay a monthly retainer for me to ideate and support every area of their growth (which often includes exposing and helping them to leverage their blind spots). I only take on ten of these clients or less at a time because they deserve my undivided attention and unwavering support.

<u>As we move forward in this book, we'll address how to create a model like this</u> that is in Alignment with your Avatar, Vision, Why, and Values. You'll learn how to develop different types of content and set pricing to meet your Avatar at their various stages of growth.

Rome wasn't built in a day, and your business won't be either. We start where you are today and naturally expand over time. Enjoy the development process (instead of pushing, forcing, squeezing, pulling, and grinding your way forward).

Q. I have two Avatars, is that ok?

A. I'm gonna force you to pick one at a time if you really have two. (But note, most people who ask me this question really only have one—just as I described above.)

Let's break this down using a doctor client of mine. He works with his patients and wants to sell them courses, supplements, books, and workshops to improve their health. He also wants to work with other practitioners to sell them certification, consulting, intensive ongoing education seminars, and the opportunity to partner in expansion.

My advice to him was to focus on the patient Avatar fully in his online platform. We revamped his branding (to evoke the emotions we knew his Avatar would want to feel), booked him a photoshoot (with images that created more connection with his Avatar), reworked his website design and copy, rebranded all of his social channels, developed a marketing content plan with topics and stories that would create engagement with his Avatar, and updated his offerings to more directly meet their needs.

As he grew his online platform, other practitioners started following him, curious about what he was doing since it all looked so effective. (And, it was!) We added a page to his website titled "For Practitioners" that had a short bit of information about his Vision in working with other doctors and invited them to contact him to start a conversation. Only when he drew enough interest did we talk about siphoning off that webpage into a secondary brand with its own Avatar, marketing, and sales operation, etc.

This is a very different scenario and strategy than the story of Heather. This is an example where the business owner had two Avatars, and because of that, over time he needed to create two separate brands in order to stay fully in Alignment and allow both to meet their potential for Infinite Impact.

Q. Won't this significantly reduce my growth potential?

A. Absolutely NOT. If anything, it will help you grow much faster and with more ease than you've previously experienced. You've probably heard the phrase, "There's riches in the niches."

Remember that even though my person is Heather, more than 70% of my clients are men. The power of the exercise is in getting clarity about the essence of your Avatar (their thoughts and feelings) as opposed to attaching a gender to it. We create a gender, age, and hair color so we may best visualize the individual we'll be talking to.

The people who resonate with my style of writing and speaking are the ones who are attracted to and choose to work with me. This book is a perfect example of that. There will be people who will be disinterested in my approach, just as there will be people who fall head over heels for it. And that's ok.

<u>I want to work with my favorite type of people to meet my needs and theirs simultaneously.</u>

<u>When I cross my own boundaries, I get smacked with a bad client experience.</u> Since I'm not keen to attract more bad experiences, I am specific about who I want to work with, use the language of my Values to attract them, and offer products and services that are in Alignment with my Foundational Four.

The next time you go to create a social media video, write a book, or prepare a speech, do it ONLY for your Avatar!

Imagine what they need to hear right now. What are they thinking and feeling?

==Get specific and share your cause with an open heart, directly to your Avatar, in full service, to help them meet their needs.==

Once you start genuinely and deeply connecting with that one person, you will look up and find everyone else around you is also feeling the difference in your content. This is precisely the time when more and more qualified leads start flowing through your business, each vocalizing how glad they are to have found you. You will actually *feel* your own Alignment, and leading your business will only get better from there.

> "I've learned that people will forget what you said, people will forget what you did, but people will never forget how you made them feel."
> – Maya Angelou

CHAPTER 6

VISION

As a business owner, you've probably heard that you should create and share your Vision because it is necessary to provide focus, clarity, and accountability in the organization.

Typical Vision statements look something like this:

1. **Google**: "To organize the world's information and make it universally accessible and useful."

2. **Tesla**: "To create the most compelling car company of the 21st century by driving the world's transition to electric vehicles."

3. **Nike**: "To bring inspiration and innovation to every athlete* in the world. (*If you have a body, you are an athlete.)"

The vast majority of business owners have lost a significant amount of time, money, and confidence by writing Vision statements about impacting a million (or a billion) lives—not realizing the implications of focusing on such an extreme goal.

Most entrepreneurs come to me with enormous goals saying their Vision is to help literally everyone. *(Or worse, they ask ME what their goals should be!)*

True story: A woman came to a strategy session with me saying she…

- Wanted to launch her book in less than two months
- MUST hit New York Times Bestseller
- Had a budget smaller than $5,000
- Knew she was meant to have a global Impact and sell many millions of copies of her book
- Was unclear about who her Avatar was because "everyone" is her Avatar.
- Had no team, no website, and no experience launching a book or marketing a cause online
- Didn't have much of a network because her book didn't have anything to do with her day job, and she didn't want to reach out to the people she did know because she hadn't been nurturing (giving to) those relationships

Do you think she had set herself up for success?

Unless she slowed down, did The Work, and methodically built her platform in Alignment, there was NO WAY she could have achieved her goals. And when an author doesn't achieve their goals, I know it's very likely that they will archive their brand, hide, and move on to try something else, cutting off any chance of Infinite Impact with that cause.

(I'm not ragging on this one woman to single her out. A LOT of people come to me in a very similar situation.)

> *You have to be responsible with your ideas and dreams. They came to you through years of learning for a very important and specific reason.*

This is an invitation for you to quit the charade and eliminate a scattered, unfocused approach. Instead, choose to build your mindset, cause, and brand purposefully and sustainably.

<u>If you could be brutally honest with yourself and get rid of what you think you "should" have a Vision for…what would you *want* to do with the remaining precious days of your life?</u>

<u>And how does that naturally pair up with *the way* and the *degree* to which you will choose to be in service to others?</u>

In the early years of growing my company, I just knew I wanted to help others feel seen, heard, and valued. However, as we started scaling quickly in 2020, I was told to create a big, hairy, audacious goal (a BHAG). My team and I played with creating a Vision statement that said we wanted to *"Be the most sought-after agency and community for Conscious Leaders who want to help course-correct humanity."* I did what I thought I was supposed to do, but in all honesty, that never really grabbed me. It sounded nice but felt a little "out there."

No wonder I had so many painful learning lessons when trying to grow my Impact…as I said, **I was out of Alignment**.

After many years of working harder and harder trying to force outcomes, I went back to the drawing board. I created my Foundational Four Framework to uncover where I had veered off the path. The exercises held me accountable, and it quickly became obvious where I was falling short. (More on that in Chapter 7.)

As it relates to Vision specifically, I saw that by going super **micro** (what we could do to help individuals) instead of **macro** (what we could do to help humanity), the Vision grabbed me in ways nothing had before. I was far more motivated, and it felt much more realistic.

The kicker? By focusing on the micro, I am more naturally achieving the macro through the ripples of Impact (with a lot less pressure and a lot more fun). Instead of grinding away, hoping "someday" you'll achieve your huge (macro) Vision, this approach provides you opportunities to achieve your (micro) Vision every single day!

So, what did I write for my micro-Vision?

My micro-Vision is to help the person who's in front of me to…

- Fully listen to their voice (intuition) and be guided by it.
- No longer be afraid to think of themselves as, or call themselves, Thought Leaders, Influencers, or Experts.
- Feel empowered, Aligned, playful, and joyful at the thought of sharing their voice through social media, stages, or in the written word.
- Trust the process and surrender expectations or "shoulds" as it relates to an outcome.
- No longer feel insecure about the way they express their cause, especially in comparison to the way others deliver content.

- Release their unhealthy attachment to follower count because they now believe that by showing up in action every day, meeting their potential, and leaving it all on the line, they will naturally achieve Infinite Impact.

- Exercise their capability, freedom, self-love, awareness, accountability, love for others, trust, kindness, effort, resilience, mindset, self-forgiveness, compassion, creativity, innovation, discipline, well-being, and gratitude.

- Move quickly, trusting their voice and letting go of the fear that they need scripts, copywriters, editors, or someone to come up with ideas for them.

- Lean into their fears, resistance, overwhelm, and confusion to experience the speed that comes from having razor-sharp clarity.

- Partner with a Books & Business strategist to ensure their organization stays in Alignment.

- Stay open and fully embrace creating meaningful connection with others even when life feels difficult.

- Have "Taylor Swift moments" regularly (in concert, Taylor pauses for several minutes to fully soak in her screaming fans). This can also look like celebrating and honoring their progress, and deeply receiving compliments and help from others.

- Let go of the idea they have to do everything themselves, and instead embrace delegating to their team and other strategic partners.

- Redefine their relationship with time and protect it from distraction and waste, in order to experience more enjoyment and fulfillment.

- Fully embrace their personal and professional value, setting healthy boundaries rooted in mutual reciprocation with others, both financially and emotionally.

Can you imagine the Impact of helping 1,000 individuals experience themselves and life that way?!

> (It is VERY doable for you to Impact one thousand people in the next decade—equivalent to talking with only two people per week through podcasts, stages, social media, and more.)

Imagine the global Impact those thousand people would have if they *each* Impacted 1,000 additional lives in the next decade. The ripple effect of your individual Impact on those 1,000 people would grow to equal one million people. That infinite reach would occur naturally *without* you having a Vision filled with pressure that creates more emotional baggage for you to carry around.

My goal is to reduce your pressure everywhere I can and to help remind you of what truly matters most to you. Only then can you experience the honest happiness and deep satisfaction that comes from living out your Vision.

Once you understand your micro-Vision and how you want to create Impact, there are three ways to grow and scale your following/prospects/reach:

1. **Organic** - An organic marketing approach is necessary (as you'll read a lot about in Chapter 10), but it is painful to solely count on it because organic marketing is highly time-consuming and yields very little result until you prove your value and consistency to algorithms and search engines over a long period of time. That's because these days, you are competing with so many other content creators for the attention of your audience. I firmly believe in the power of organic but advise my clients to view it as a way that "referral prospects" can validate their credibility and trustworthiness, rather than relying solely on it to generate a high volume of leads in the first few years.

2. **Paid** - The paid advertising approach is enormously expensive, requires a unicorn team, and generates a large, mostly unqualified community who rarely buy products or services that offer meaningful value. There is a very specific group of internet marketers who use paid advertising to drive leads into a low-entry funnel offering more generic how-to content. Their general strategy is to make a lot of small, incremental sales versus what you and I are here to do, which is to create meaningful connection and lasting transformation. Of course, there are no absolutes, but most entrepreneurs will fall into one of these traps at one point or another in their growth journey.

3. **1:1** (which feeds into Organic) - Lots of strategies can generate an *immediate* community that you can connect to and collaborate with to quickly grow your reach and revenue. Through that small community's referrals, you'll have a growing number of *qualified* individuals who visit your organic

social presence to validate that you are someone credible and trustworthy. These individuals will buy your products and services that offer meaningful value to them and, in turn, refer additional qualified individuals, which consistently and sustainably scales the growth of your brand.

It's MUCH easier for a new brand to focus (or an established brand to re-focus) on 1:1 Impact as a long-term scaling-up strategy versus playing the organic or paid advertising game up front, hoping to strike gold and grow a big following.

Most people grind and push and force and pull only to vent in frustration that "it's" not working ("it's" = book/brand/cause/offer/branding/strategy).

You might blame your marketing team or a peer who gave you bad advice when really, you just don't know what you don't know about how the online marketplace operates as a whole.

I started my company 17 years ago, which means I've observed and participated in the development of how online marketing and online brand growth works.

By eliminating the over-saturation of hacks being spewed in your social media feed, and instead going inward to tap in to your unique genius, then sharing that with a giving heart to the one person in front of you... you'll find that the way forward was available to you all along.

You'll experience the Impact of one person here and one person there. You'll form *genuine* bonds whether someone buys from you immediately or waits until the timing is right for them. After experiencing your presence and care, those individuals will then inevitably tell others about how special you are, and magic starts brewing around you.

Then, you'll want to keep this 1:1 strategy going.

The temptation you'll face is to layer on paid ads to throw gasoline on the fire. **Caution!** To break down your logic: You're taking time and energy *away* from a *working strategy* to layer on an unproven, costly, new strategy. I emphasize this now because this decision can easily get you out of Alignment and into a loop of destruction. I'm not saying there isn't a time and place for paid ads. I'm just saying it's not early on in brand development. Don't be so quick to busy yourself with additional strategies and pressure.

(To be clear, I've worked with multiple brands who had accumulated 1,000,000 email subscribers—a seemingly mature brand—who I would still classify as being "early on" in their brand development because of how out of Alignment their brands actually were. They had lost the intimate feeling of meaningful connection with members of their community and needed a strategy to regroup, refocus, and market in a more Aligned way. Once that happened, magic appeared!)

Before piling on new strategies, stick with the 1:1 strategy for longer than you think you should to really grow the compound effect of referrals. Listen to both the needs and the praise of the small group in front of you. Keep giving to them. Keep nurturing the people closest to you, and watch your Impact grow even more.

Focus on what you can give to the people in front of you versus focusing on what new followers, numbers, or data you can get.

Before you know it, you'll have energy and excitement flowing steadily around you in your business. And then you'll notice your following start to grow organically even though you weren't grinding, pushing, and forcing. You'll notice you aren't so frustrated and things just seem to be working.

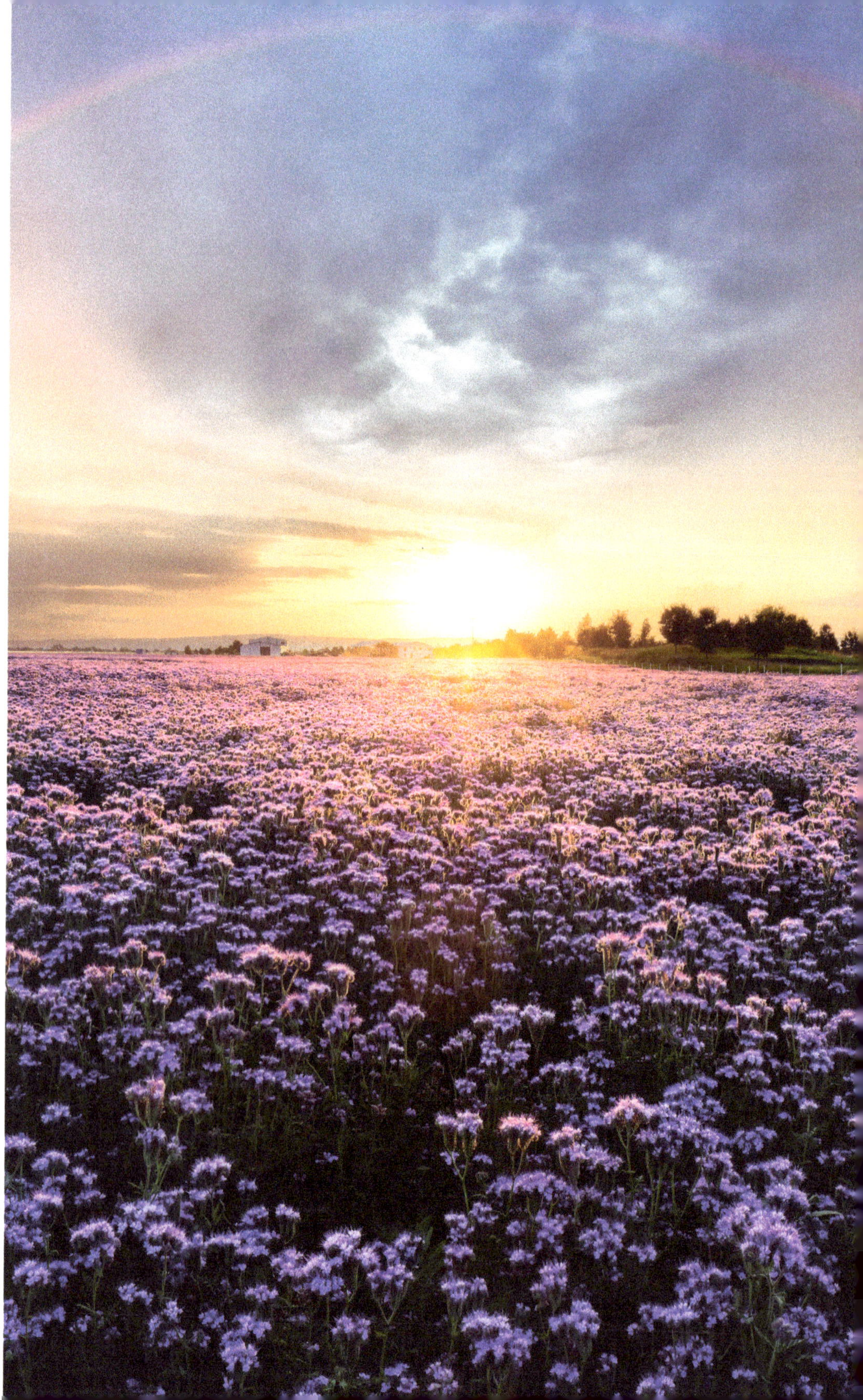

VISION EXERCISE

I'm now going to guide you through the same exercise that has been such a game-changer for me and so many of my clients. I'm going to give you instructions, support you with writing prompts, offer troubleshooting, and then follow up with action steps for your team.

The work you do here will set you up for *great* success in Part 3 when we work to create harmony in your marketing, sales, and operations, allowing you to achieve your Vision more quickly and with more enjoyment.

> **ENTREPRENEUR ACTION, STEP 1:**

With your Avatar in mind, write your micro-Vision in the space below.

Writing prompts:

- ☐ How will this individual think differently?
- ☐ How will their connection improve with their family and/or spouse?
- ☐ What fears or challenges will they overcome?
- ☐ What positive emotions will they experience moving forward?
- ☐ What will they experience spiritually?
- ☐ How will their mindset change?
- ☐ What will they do to give back to others, to pay it forward?
- ☐ What will they have redefined in their lives?
- ☐ What will they release or let go of?
- ☐ How will their confidence/love/results improve?

- ☐ How will their quality of life change (sleep, self-love, financial abundance, etc.)?
- ☐ What will they stop doing?
- ☐ What will they be inspired to do differently?
- ☐ What will they be thanking you for?
- ☐ What will they do more of? Less of?

<u>My Vision is to help the person in front of me to...</u>

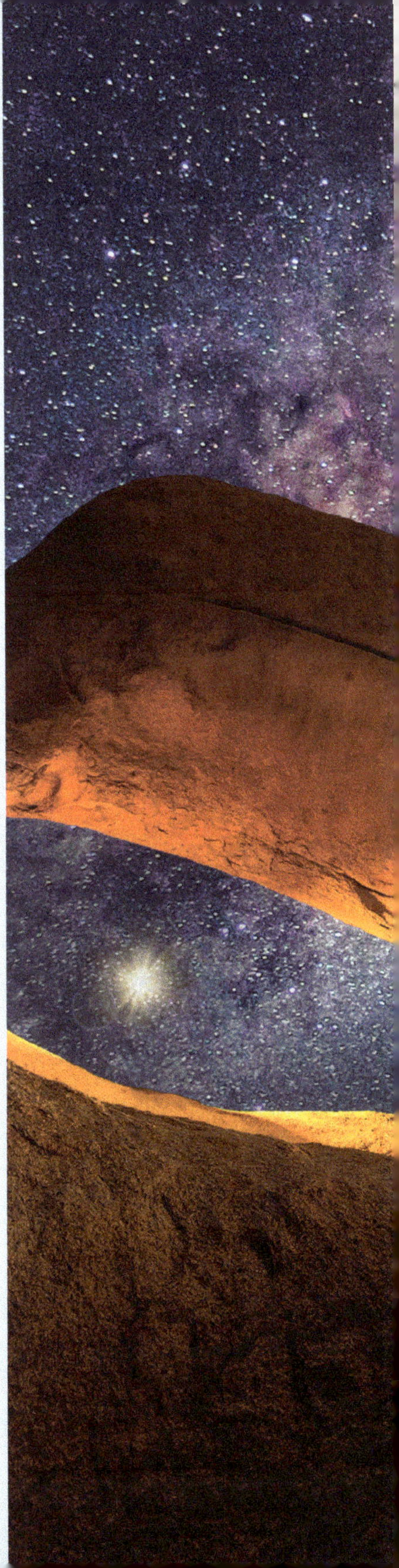

Troubleshooting:

1. It can help to think of people you've helped in the past, whether a neighbor, client, child, or friend. What did you say or do that helped them? What was the outcome?

2. Now, imagine one person in front of you who you really want to Impact in a positive way—your Avatar. Think about what they experience day-to-day, what they need most from you, and how they will feel on the other side of that change.

3. Think of the specific praise you have received in the past from testimonials, or as people have made introductions to you. How do people describe you, and how did they come to believe that?

4. Note: This is an exercise involving your heart more than your mind. What change do you want to see in the world, one person at a time?

Once you have your micro-Vision list in a "good enough" place (80% or more congruent), the next step is to distill that into one sentence.

For example:

> My Vision is to help individuals feel seen, heard, and valued.

(Commit this to memory because I refer to it a lot in future chapters.)

That is a summation of my full list of micro-Vision goals.

Look at how *doable* that is compared to: "Be the most sought-after agency and community for Conscious Leaders who want to help course-correct humanity."

If **my new focus** is to help each individual I'm in front of feel seen, heard, and valued, my success rate will climb through the roof! My confidence and sense of deep fulfillment scales with it.

Your turn.

ENTREPRENEUR ACTION, STEP 2:

Write your distilled Vision statement in the space below (the summation of your micro-Vision goals).

_____

_____

As a business owner, you can now keep that Vision in mind as you make decisions about your:

- Team experience
- Customer journey
- Branding look and feel
- Website layout
- Social media captions
- Sales pitch

- Customer experience
- Book content experience
- Network collaborations
- And more

...All of which will be discussed throughout the rest of this book!

Going one step deeper, you'll want to keep that Vision in mind when you think about <u>what *you* need to show up as your highest and best self</u> so you are better equipped to achieve that Vision.

For example, to help individuals feel seen, heard, and valued, I need to be rested, be excited, be focused, have mental clarity, be open, have a loving spirit, be focused on giving instead of getting, be optimistic, etc.

ENTREPRENEUR ACTION, STEP 3:

List what you need to successfully bring your Vision to fruition:

Writing prompts:

- ☐ What will you need to feel?
- ☐ What state of mind would you need to be in?
- ☐ What kind of rest or play will that require?
- ☐ How can your family support you?
- ☐ What environment do you need to be in?
- ☐ What physical, emotional, or spiritual state might you need to be in?
- ☐ Where would you need to go? What would you need to do?
- ☐ What does your team or culture need to look like?
- ☐ What relationships would you need to develop and nurture?
- ☐ What accountability pieces would need to be in place?
- ☐ How can your team support you?

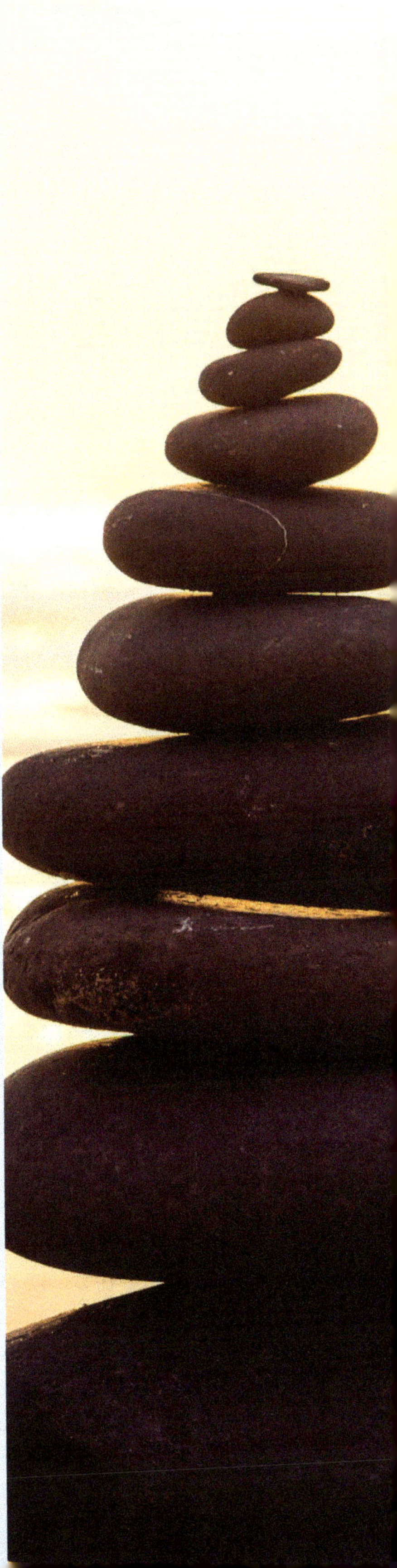

Troubleshooting:

1. If, for example, you need to be "optimistic" to fulfill your Vision... go one step deeper and determine what needs to happen for you to feel optimistic vs. pessimistic.

    a. For example, when I watch the news, I often feel pessimistic. Therefore, I would need to make a conscious choice not to watch the news, or limit my intake, so that I maintain my optimism about life and helping others.

2. Think about day-to-day distractions that could knock you off course.

    a. For example, if rushing out of the house to drop the kids at school knocks you off course, you could set up a different morning routine (such as making lunches the night before) so you aren't rushed getting out the door.

3. Think about the relationships in your life that create the most friction or frustration. What is the opposite you would need to feel empowered and joyful?
    a. For example, if a family member doesn't respect your work and that leaves you feeling disempowered, the flip side of that is that you need to be surrounded by people who believe in and appreciate your work.
    b. Then you can think about boundaries to put in place for the downers in your life who are there to stay (such as not discussing work projects with them anymore).
4. Think about your shadow habits or outlets and how those take you away from being your best self. (By "shadow," I mean the less prized things you use to escape or numb. No judgment here. Is it binge-watching TV, gaming, drinking, etc?) If those habits start to get in the way of you fulfilling your Vision (e.g., drinking too much and waking up hungover, therefore less motivated to help others), then it's time to create accountability measures so you stop after two drinks instead of going for five. This could be phoning a friend, rewarding yourself for sticking to two, etc.

By completing this simple exercise, you're now able to:

- Reframe your goal from "helping everyone" into a more tangible and realistic Vision.

- Release unnecessary pressure and emotional baggage from pushing for and not achieving something you weren't really that attached to from the beginning.

- Define *how* you want to specifically and profoundly Impact individuals.

- Approach your marketing and sales strategy in stronger Alignment, which will produce a more accurate roadmap to achieve your Vision faster.

- Experience a more natural energy toward growth.

- Stay focused on the 1:1 connection exchange that is the most overlooked (yet most powerful) strategy in marketing.

This is just the *beginning* of the power this book is going to offer you.

> *At the end of the day, even if you have a clear and compelling Vision, your WHY must be bigger than the many distractions fighting to get you off course.*

While your Vision is centered around what your company/cause will do for **others**, my take is that your Why should be centered around what your company/cause will do for **you**. The mutual reciprocation flowing between your Vision and Why creates an unmatched harmony that scales your brand while offering you personal freedom and fulfillment.

Before we address your Why in the next chapter, we must Align your team around your Vision.

Remember, you're not alone. You have people in your corner who will help you.

You've heard the phrase that we are only as strong as our weakest link? That's why it's so critical to get every employee, contractor, *and vendor* on the same page to fiercely protect your Vision and ensure the organization is held to the highest possible standards of excellence.

As discussed in the Introduction, if you're just starting your business and don't have a team yet, that is 100% ok. The action I suggest is that you hire a **Creative Marketing Assistant (CMA)** to start collaborating with. To support you in that, your Toolkit offers a job description, as well as hiring and training support.

If you already have a team, you might feel some initial resistance to sharing your thoughts and feelings with them as The Work continues. That's totally understandable. The old way of doing business taught us that it might not be safe or "appropriate" to be vulnerable.

However, a new way is emerging out of the realization that unless those closest to you can connect with you and your Why on a deeper level, their natural gifts and talents won't be fully activated to help you achieve your Vision. You can achieve far more productivity and better retention when you have an Aligned team that has bought into WHO YOU ARE and what you are here to bring to the world.

Therefore, having the courage to share *openly* and *honestly* will breed connection, and you will get more of what you want out of your team in return.

TEAM ACTION LIST:

1. Read this chapter carefully and think about what additional ideas you can add to your leader's micro-Vision list.

2. In your observation, what can *you* do in your role to hold the organization accountable to this Vision? What might get in your team's way? How can you overcome that quickly?

3. Fill out the worksheet in your Workbook (found in the Toolkit at www.InfiniteImpactBook.com) that formalizes the primary Vision statement and total micro-Vision list.

4. Suggest the use of the Vision worksheet as an accountability tool company-wide to ensure the brand is presented accurately to prospects throughout your online platform. By marketing the company well, you'll see sales growth with qualified customers. This can also be used as an accountability tool in your culture. Bring any concerns to your leader immediately if something is off or not working as harmoniously as you think it could.

    Pro Tip: When communicating concerns with your leader, share with them how you came to believe that to be true or what insights you have, tie it back to their Vision, then offer a few suggestions and solutions so they are not alone in figuring out what to do with this information. You will be viewed as more valuable to the company, which can support your long-term growth potential.

5. Encourage the scheduling of a company-wide quarterly meeting to review your Vision document and openly address any areas where you've fallen off track, and what accountability ideas the group has to stay Aligned for the quarter ahead.

SUMMARY OF YOUR PROGRESS

You are doing The Work in preparation for being seen and heard so you are ready for Infinite Impact. You are clear on your Avatar and how you want to Impact that person (Vision), and have accountability measures in place to give you the best chance at success.

Next up, you will:

1. Explore and lock in your Why using an exercise framework I developed that has already changed *many* lives in a very positive way.

2. Revisit and redefine your Values more deeply than you might have considered before so you have unwavering conviction in your boundaries and attract the right, qualified individuals into your community.

Remember, this is an extremely important time to get, and stay, in Alignment. Along with the tremendous technological advances we've experienced in our lifetime came a tsunami of competition (even though I don't like that word). As more and more individuals are listening to the calling to create a positive shift in the world, on top of all of the individuals who contribute straight-up noise, it has never been more difficult to market your cause. For many years I've talked about how to win the attention game online, and that was *before* the rise of AI. We are experiencing an entirely new era now and are likely in for some real surprises.

Your best move is to settle in and get very, very clear on what exactly it is that you want out of your Vision. Then, use the results you'll get from the next two chapters to go out and grow your Aligned tribe.

As you meet each new person who Aligns with your Vision and Why, spend your days focused on them, nurturing them, and showing up for them in big ways. Allow a bit of time and space for those deposits to grow and come back to you with significant interest.

Don't be too quick to layer on new, unproven strategies. Keep anchoring your actions to your Vision. When you find something that works (especially at a small level), KEEP GOING. Go micro.

Once you have established your Vision, locking in your Why will bring about renewed passion, meaning, and direction in your life. Flip the page, and let's get started!

> "I alone cannot change the world,
> but I can cast a stone across the waters
> to create many ripples."
> - Mother Teresa

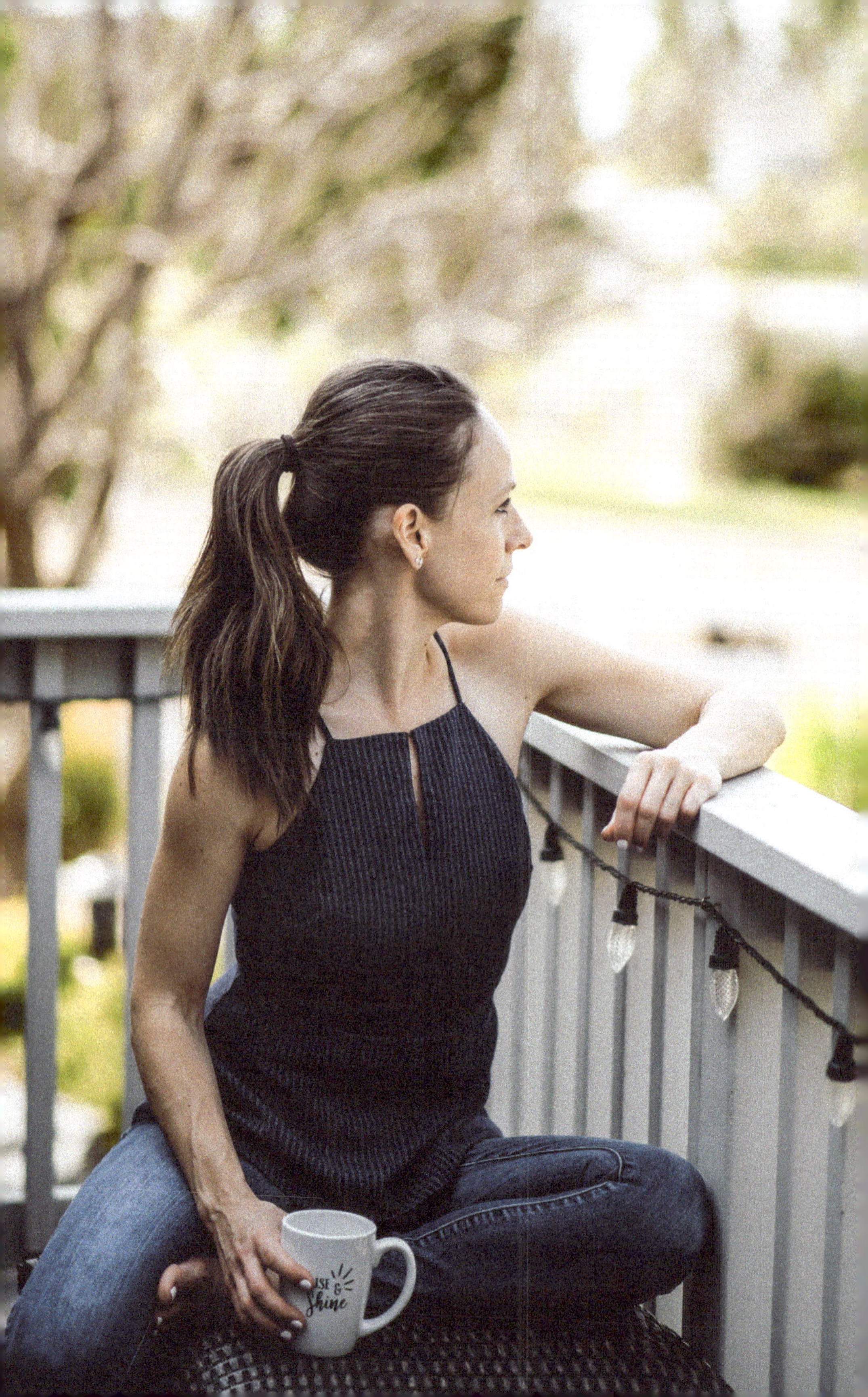
ISE &
Shine

CHAPTER 7

WHY

I lost my Why.

I didn't know where I'd lost it, or when exactly during the pandemic, but it was gone.

I felt isolated, confused, hurt, and scared.

After the jarring awareness that I was disconnected from my Why, I began asking anyone in front of me what their Why was. I figured maybe it would awaken my sleeping giant. After all, I'm a mountain mover. I'm the one you call when you *think* you're operating in Alignment, yet aren't because you can't see your own blind spots. I'm the one who helps others get their mojo back. But this felt…different.

Days turned into weeks, and I sat in the discomfort of my own query. An invisible box of my own design.

I wondered if I would ever get it back—ever feel the passion that helped me shape industries and countless lives.

Grief has a strange way of sideswiping us. It feeds off the remains of whatever it didn't already rob from you. It creeps in, then hits you with a deafening boom when you least expect it. It slows your momentum. And if it slows you for too long, doubt takes root and starts to grow, spreading like a toxic weed, threatening to take you down.

It's hard to run a business, a team, a movement…when we feel lost.

We fight a strong battle of competing needs. One side wants to maximize every second, get over it, and just move forward. The other begs to hide, needing an autumn and winter to regroup.

<u>Deep in contemplation during my brief respite, clichés were loud in my head:</u>

- Get comfortable with being uncomfortable.
- Embrace the unknown.
- Live your best life.
- Time heals all wounds.
- Beauty is in the eye of the beholder.
- You get to choose your experience.
- Each day is a new opportunity to try again.

In that space, it's painful to watch what appears like everyone else living their best lives. Social media can be a serious trap when you're lost. Yet, because we seek clues for our next best move, we scroll and scroll, searching for inspiration only to close the app, usually feeling worse.

→ **When you know your Why**, you feel on top of the world. Your passion ignites an internal fire in the people you meet. You have boundless energy and focus. Every day feels like play. More and more people gravitate to spend time in your orbit.

→ **When you've lost your Why**, you feel like a giant loser. You collect evidence for how little you know and determine it's best just to keep quiet and wait until the tides turn. You spend your days distracted, ruminating on the source of your discomfort. At best, you feel inadequate and unfulfilled; at worst, you see yourself as a fraud.

Your Why is a deeply personal thing. You are the only person who can unlock your Why (...and keep it that way).

I knew that I'd lost my Why and that I needed to redefine it.

Notice I didn't say "get it back."

==When you disconnect with your Why, it's because the season of that Why has come to an end.==

You don't have just one Why for the entirety of your life. You are a human evolving every minute of every day. Usually, a Why expires when there's an invitation to go deeper to redefine a more true Why that leads to self-actualization.

When you experience growth sprints, you shed the old skin of who you were to stretch into the higher and better version of yourself. Your company does the same.

Your Why deepens, your Vision expands, and the business model must evolve to stay in Alignment.

Your Why *is not* **something as simple and obvious as: "To help as many people as possible"** *(...which is what people usually tell me on strategy calls)*. And it's not something like, "I want to make a lot of money to be financially free."

Go deeper. *Why* is that your Why?

Imagine an onion. You need to peel back a layer to see what's beneath, then another layer and another layer. I want you to keep going deeper and deeper into your Why until you fully understand what drives your decisions. (Hint: You have an unmet need trying to be filled.) In order to do this, we will expand on your discoveries from the Chapter 3 Course-Correction exercise.

In order to find your Why, most thought leaders suggest you reflect on your Values, personal motivations, and long-term Vision. I wholeheartedly agree. However, often their next suggested step is to define your Why in a statement that can very closely resemble your Vision statement.

I thought I had been living my Why…being in service to others. But I discovered that I had only been pursuing my Vision.

I propose that while your Vision is anchored in what your company/cause will do for others, your Why should be anchored in what your company/cause will do for you.

Put another way, your Vision meets the needs of your Tribe, and your Why meets your own personal needs.

==When your Vision and Why intertwine, mutual reciprocation occurs, and that's when you will experience the kind of harmony in your life and business that is extremely attractive to others. This congruence resonates at the strongest levels, and growth in sales and Impact is the natural result.==

Mutual reciprocation is a foundational principle that nature teaches us.

- Earth provides nutrients to a majestic tree that in exchange cleans our air and provides live-giving qualities back to the planet and all who inhabit it.
- Bees and butterflies pollinate flowers, which facilitates the reproduction of plants and trees, and in exchange, pollinators receive nourishment that enables their growth and sustainability.
- A coral reef offers protection to an abundance of marine life, while the fish and sea creatures contribute to its overall health and diversity.

It's time to bring this ancient wisdom into our businesses and offer a far more enriched and fulfilling experience to each person who interacts with the brand.

As someone who didn't know how to receive (and instead focused on giving…), this was much easier said than done. Or so I initially thought.

WHAT DO YOU DO IF YOU'VE LOST YOUR WHY (...OR NEVER REALLY KNEW IT IN THE FIRST PLACE)?

In *Start with Why*, Simon Sinek writes, "Before it can gain any power or achieve any impact, an arrow must be pulled backward, 180 degrees away from the target. And that's also where a WHY derives its power. The WHY does not come from looking ahead at what you want to achieve and figuring out an appropriate strategy to get there."

Ouch. Accountability smacked me right in the face when I read that. As a strategist, this is exactly what I have done in the past. I knew I wanted to help people, so I designed a strategy that did exactly that. But at the end of the day, it wasn't reciprocal and I was burning out from giving all of myself away to others every day. I needed to go deeper and learn how to meet my own needs while also helping others meet theirs.

Sinek continues, "It is not born out of any market research. It does not come from extensive interviews with customers or even employees. It comes from looking in the complete opposite direction from where you are now. Finding WHY is a process of discovery, not invention."

If I needed to look in the complete opposite direction of where I was (looking outward to help others), that meant I needed to look inward and figure out what I was missing in order to redefine my Why. *That's when something clicked and I knew just what to do next!*

I went back to the Courage to Course-Correct exercise and used that process to help me:

1. **IDENTIFY.** Instead of listing my resistance, I listed my greatest desires in life.
2. **EXPLORE.** I searched for what created those desires to begin with (my unmet needs—feelings I didn't get enough of as a kid or adult).
3. **EVALUATE.** I looked at where those unmet needs got me in life. (Spoiler alert: it held me back.)
4. **SHIFT.** And finally, I built my Why to not only meet my needs but also create the congruence I needed to create Infinite Impact.

I was blown away by the incredible bounty this exercise ended up giving me. Empowerment, personal freedom, peace of mind, increased financial success, deeper connection with others… This just names a few of the benefits of getting into Alignment. I can't wait for you to experience it yourself!

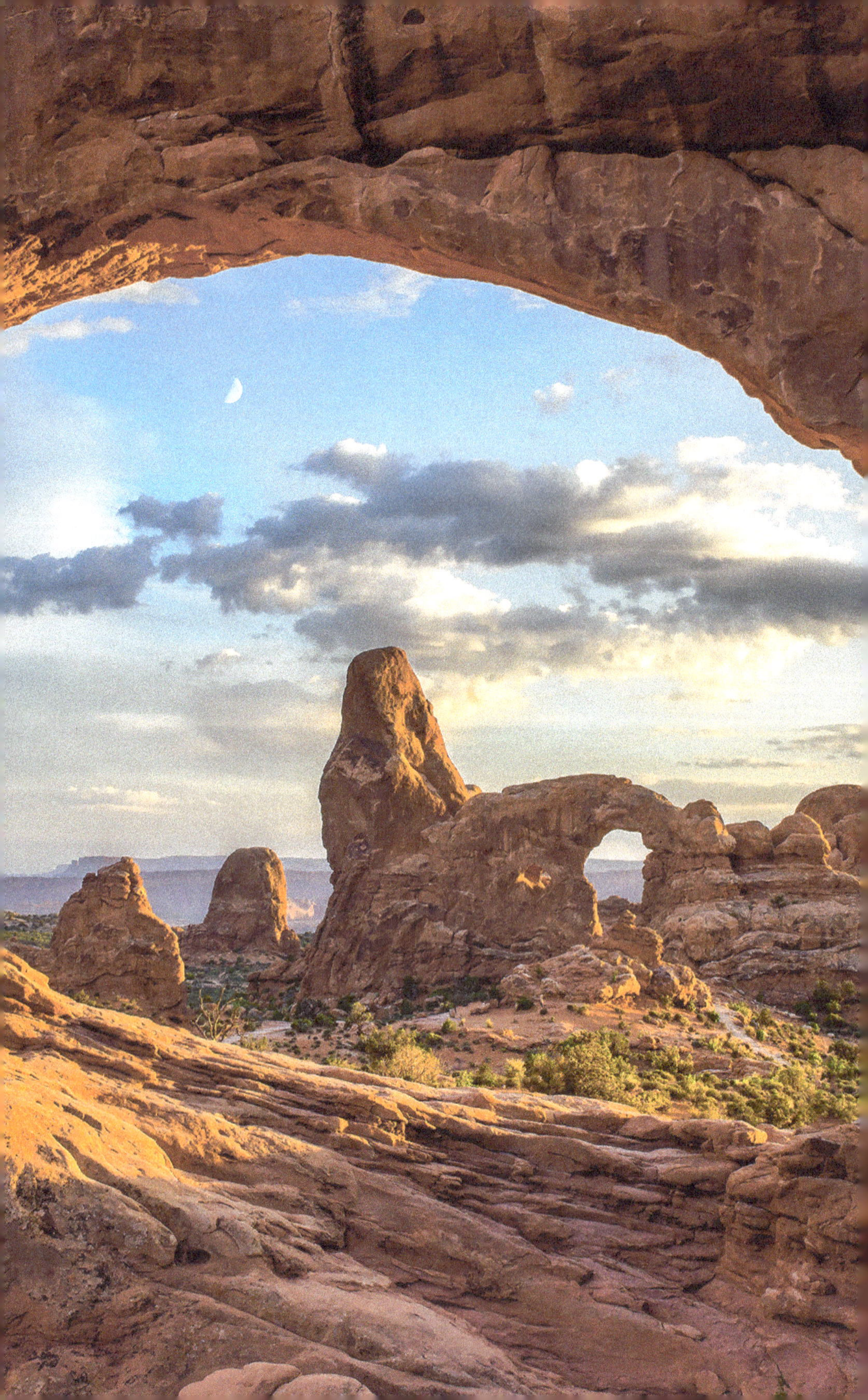

WHY EXERCISE

In order to design your Why in a way that meets your own needs (a necessary reciprocation from giving to others), let's get playful and first look at what you most want to feel and experience in life.

I'm **not** talking about what you want to *obtain* such as cars, money, homes, or retirement. When your Why is centered around tangible things like a boat, farm, finding your soulmate, or achieving a certain amount of savings, you're likely to find emptiness in the achievement because you'll still live with deeper "unmet needs."

Our aim with this exercise is to address our most desired *intangible* needs such as love, trust, protection, belonging, respect, intimacy, etc. What do you want most…so badly that you would give almost anything to experience it *genuinely*?

ENTREPRENEUR ACTION, STEP 1 [IDENTIFY]:

Make a list of roughly 10-15 things you most want to feel and experience in your future.

Writing prompts:

- ☐ How do you want others to feel about you?
- ☐ How do you want to feel about yourself?
- ☐ What did you experience as a kid, and what would you choose to experience instead as an adult?
- ☐ What is one of the most hurtful things you've endured, and what is the opposite of that?

- ☐ Identify a habit or pattern you are trying to break, and list the outcome you want instead.
- ☐ Consider what you would want most for your child, spouse, or friend, and list those best wishes for them.
- ☐ Imagine a child who has been emotionally wounded, abandoned, misunderstood, or rejected; what would you wish for them instead?
- ☐ What life lessons have you learned or are you still learning?

I want to...

Troubleshooting:

1. It can help to think of what you do NOT want moving forward. Then flip that and write the opposite.

    a. As an example, if I don't want to be rejected, instead I want to be accepted. Or, if I don't want to be codependent, instead I want to be autonomous. Or, if I am sick of feeling incompetent (imposter syndrome), then instead I'd want to know I am capable.

2. Consider what emotions you want to feel.

    a. For example, you may want to feel empowered, joyful, and grateful. Then consider what would need to happen to feel like that every day.

3. Sometimes, it's too difficult to examine our own experience. In those cases, it can help to think of well wishes you have for friends or family members instead, then use those ideas to map your own desires.

As I did the exercise, I wrote this list in my journal:

- Know the truth.
- Use my voice.
- Move through my fears.
- Do something that matters. Something significant.
- Know my life mattered.
- Be chosen.
- Be seen.
- Be heard.
- Be connected.
- Be protected.
- Be valued.
- Be a protector for others who are being bullied or misunderstood.
- Surround myself with people who advocate for me to open up and experience freedom.

- Stand up for myself.
- Love myself fully.
- Not be edited.

> ### ENTREPRENEUR ACTION, STEP 1B:

Now go back and circle or highlight the top five desires that have the strongest pull, and put a star next to your "core" (primary) desire.

I narrowed my list down to:
- **Know the truth.** *(My core desire.)*
- Move through my fears.
- Do something that matters. Something significant.
- Be seen.
- Be heard.

Debrief: This list comes from decades of life experiences where the opposite was my reality. **Therefore, what I wanted most for my future actually stemmed from a core need I didn't get enough of growing up.**

As you focus on your top desires, allow yourself to get curious about where those desires stem from. The answers may already be obvious to you, but what helped me was to look at the opposite of each desire and reflect on memories that were tied to an old core limiting belief.

In my experience, I wanted to "know the truth" because the truth was often manipulated and I didn't know what to believe growing up. I wanted to "be seen" because I often felt invisible, and I wanted to "be heard" because I often felt silenced.

Instead of going through all five of your top desires, let's focus our work here on the **core desire** you starred above.

ENTREPRENEUR ACTION, STEP 2 [EXPLORE]:

Start by writing your core desire in the section below, then flip it to write your core belief.

*(If, for example, your **core desire** is "to be protected," flip that to list the **core belief** as "I am not protected.")*

My core desire is to… _____
_____(now flip it) and that comes from the core belief that I… _____
_____
_____.

Next, follow any feelings that come up and trace them back to times you remember feeling that way. Itemize a few memories that contributed to the creation of that belief.

(For example, perhaps you were alone in your house at night, or a sibling didn't stand up for you, or a parent was late picking you up from school.)

ENTREPRENEUR ACTION, STEP 2B [EXPLORE]:

Memories that helped form that belief:

_____
_____
_____
_____
_____
_____

Troubleshooting:

1. This exercise may take a little time, and that's ok; *take the time you need*.

2. A friendly reminder: The goal of this exercise is not to uproot your deepest traumas and create more fear or sadness. The goal is to examine the memories that come most quickly to mind in an objective manner as if you are studying a grasshopper's steps as it's walking around in a jar. If strong emotions do show up, simply take note of them, breathe in deeply, and, as you slowly exhale, allow the emotion to pass. Do this as many times as you need to until you are ready to refocus on the exercise. Whatever you do, don't avoid what comes up for you, shut the process down, or close the book and do something else out of avoidance.

3. Also, remember that you experienced these moments when you were younger and didn't have all the information or tools to properly see all perspectives. You likely misinterpreted some

things. Regardless, remember that the purpose of this exercise is to expose what's holding you back so you gain faster and stronger momentum toward achieving Impact (which, again, is what you want *more* than you want to close the book and avoid this work).

Now that we've identified your core belief, let's look at the unmet need from which all of this grows.

*(For example, if your **core belief** is "I am not protected" then you have an **unmet need** for "protection" … you likely felt disconnected from a primary caregiver.)*

ENTREPRENEUR ACTION, STEP 2C:

Write your primary unmet need.

My core belief is that I… _____
_____ and my unmet need is for… _____
_____
_____.

ENTREPRENEUR ACTION, STEP 3 [EVALUATE]:

Write out where your core belief got you in life. You'll initially see the impact in your relationships (parents, spouse, etc.), but your unmet need is also connected to ways you robbed/betrayed yourself:

(For example, if your root belief is "I am not protected," then you may have been guarded, closed, or resistant to emotional connection. Explore past conflicts and see the role you played in them, then explore how you treated yourself. You are likely to find you were closed to providing for your own needs, or closed off from your emotions and intuition. You might have even unintentionally put pressure on others to show up in protection for you.)

Writing prompts:

- ☐ See the direct impact of that belief (following the example above, that you were not protected—therefore you want to experience protection moving forward). You'll see where this belief holds you back personally and professionally, as well as where it conflicts with who you want to be and how you want to show up in the world.
- ☐ Think about arguments you've had with a family member, spouse, or past work relationship. What behaviors showed up that contributed to its challenges?
- ☐ When we're in the presence of children, we can't hide. So, consider your level of presence and engagement with your children or other children in your life. Are you open, or do you hold them at a distance emotionally?
- ☐ Have you experienced resistance to decisions or expression out of that belief?
- ☐ Consider when you are agitated and map what triggered that reaction.
- ☐ Explore how you treated yourself out of having that root belief.
  - ☐ For example, I truly believed I couldn't fully trust loved ones around me. Upon further reflection, I found this stemmed from a lack of trusting myself. By not trusting myself, I gave away my power to others to make decisions for me. (There's the fawning again from Chapter 2.) When you do The Work, you see that it's all connected. And the beautiful thing is that with this awareness comes the ability to choose what to think and do differently moving forward.

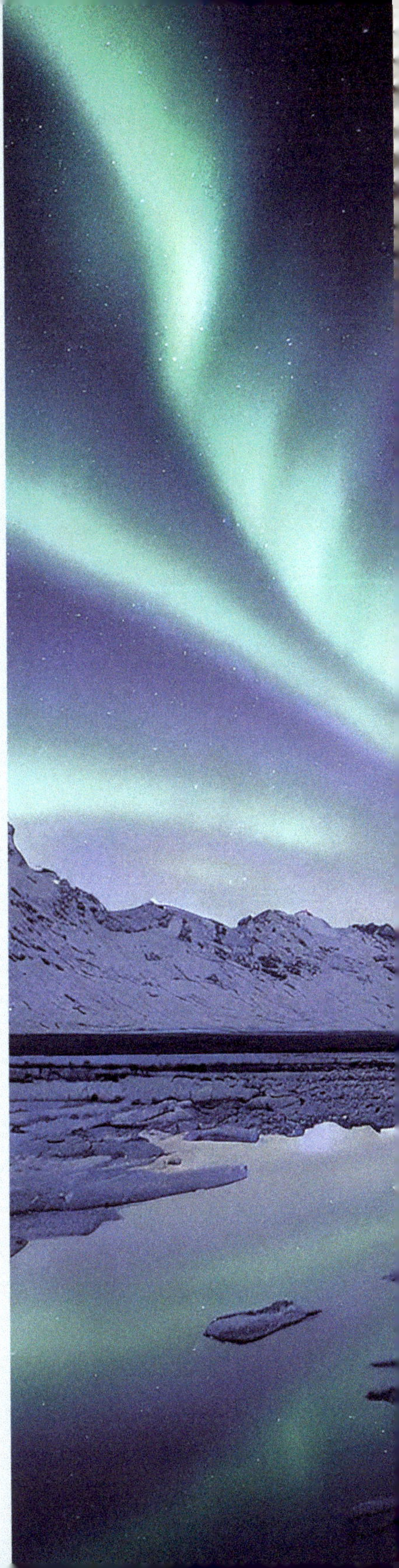

Troubleshooting:

1. Reviewing the exercise from Chapter 3 enabled me to go deeper with this one. You might find it helpful to refer back to your earlier work if you get stuck.

2. I also explored escapism. (Escapism can start innocently with binging TV, then avoiding calls and communication, then escalates to avoiding responsibility and making up for it at the last minute, drinking more, over-snacking, keeping secrets, and then gets more extreme with creating almost second lives where people have affairs, form serious addictions, and more.) Escapism—in whatever way you experience it—is very common, but shouldn't be labeled as normal. It comes from the avoidance of pain from an unmet need. For example, if I have an experience that taps into the belief that I am not protected, the pain will start to bubble up, and the knee-jerk reaction is to escape into a TV series, or snack when no one is

looking, etc. My dad always said, "Do things in moderation," and when I fall outside of that, it's an indication to pay attention. By looking at our own version of escapism, we can track the experiences, relationships, or internal dialogue that it stems from.

Debrief: Let's break down this exercise:

If your **core desire** is to be protected…it is natural that your **core belief** would be "I am not protected."

→ That core belief was formed through multiple experiences where you may have felt disconnected, inadequate, and undisciplined (unmet needs). You are likely currently getting clues to these unmet needs through work and relationship challenges.

→ In Step 4 below, we will shift to meeting your needs through your Why statement(s). Following this example, your **Why statement** would be "I want to feel protected."

- *Notice how your core desires stem directly from your unmet needs, which ultimately determines your Why statement.*

→ As you move forward in your Books & Business, you'll want to have heightened awareness of your natural focus on creating connection with others because what we give is what we need most. You give protection, you feel connection. That makes you feel protected and your **core desire** is achieved. Mutual reciprocation naturally occurs between fulfilling your Vision and receiving your Why. Congruence is present.

The same is true for me. After doing The Work, I saw that my **Vision** was to help others feel seen, heard, and valued. That is what my cause will do for *others*. What I want (my **Why**) is to feel seen, heard, and valued in return. That is what my cause will do for *me*.

My momentum in the exercise was exhilarating. My intuition communicated the insight that our Vision and Why are meant to be reciprocal, and the next thing I knew, I started making connections between my needs and desires that I'd never made before. I felt the fog starting to clear. My blind spots were being exposed, and I knew there was incredible power on the other side of this process.

There is just one more step for you to do before the metaphorical arrow is ready to launch forward, and that is to lock in your Why.

ENTREPRENEUR ACTION, STEP 4 [SHIFT]:

We will now come full circle to write your Why statements. On the left column, re-write your top five core desires for easy reference. On the right column, write out your correlating Why statements.

(For example, on the left column, write your core desire "to be protected." On the right column, write your Why statement of "I want to feel protected.")

CORE DESIRES	WHY STATEMENTS
_____	_____
_____	_____
_____	_____
_____	_____
_____	_____
_____	_____
_____	_____

Yours does not need to follow that format at all. You can map all five of your core desires or just one. You might have one sentence, or you might write a manifesto. This is why we spent so much time talking about intuition—let it be your guide. Trust yourself, and let your writing flow. Don't hold back. The Aligned Why statement will come to you, and until then, feel free to borrow from the examples above.

ENTREPRENEUR ACTION, STEP 4B [SHIFT]:

As a bonus, feel free to take this one step further by brainstorming 5-10 ideas of actions you can take to meet your own needs and experience your Why on a daily basis.

(For example, if your Why is "I want to feel protected," you can slightly alter that to read "I protect myself." Ways you can achieve that is by trusting your intuition, practicing self-care, setting healthy boundaries, sticking up for yourself, putting an end to self-deprecating behavior, weeding out relationships that aren't mutually reciprocating, etc.)

When you meet your own needs and live your Why—when you value yourself—resistance fades significantly. You'll no longer feel dissatisfied. Instead, you'll experience your uniqueness, significance, self-expression, and Impact *in ways you've never imagined.*

> What started as "I want to know the truth" led me to see that inside of me is the ultimate truth. And as long as I see/hear myself, I will feel connected to myself (and stop desperately seeking it from everyone else), I will experience value in myself, and be whole. I will have met my needs and experienced my Why.
>
> Inevitably, because I'm human, I'll backslide. (In Chapter 12, you'll witness a very recent example of this.) There will come

another day when I don't listen to my intuition, which will leave me feeling disconnected. I won't feel valued and I won't feel whole. I'll have unmet needs, and through subconscious patterning, I'll start seeking connection outside of myself to fill the void.

UNTIL I remember I've already done The Work and can just refer back to it I'll tap into my Courage to Course-Correct to get back in Alignment and keep shining my light in a natural, genuine, and harmonious way, to create Infinite Impact.

YOUR WHY GIVES YOUR BUSINESS MEANING

It's NOT just business. It's personal.

I am fully aware there are lots of individuals who operate differently. They are in a different stage of their journey, and there is nothing wrong with that.

In my experience, people are so desensitized that they're on information overload, they're exhausted, pressures have never been higher, and they're desperately searching for meaning.

==By doing The Work, you are tapping into DEEP meaning and will soon share that with everyone around you.==

Your family, friends, and community at large will resonate with your meaning. You will experience the power of word of mouth in ways you never knew possible. And, you'll be ready to be seen and heard.

As you move forward, if you ever wonder what direction to head in or what goal you should have…come back and reconnect with your Why.

A lot of people have asked me what vitamins I take, or what I eat, simply because they want to know how I have so much energy to be so highly productive.

Well, I'll tell you, it comes from a very natural place because I am Aligned, and I'm very clear on who my Avatar is as well as what my Vision, Why, and Values are (which is what we get to dig into next!).

The Foundational Four Framework offers you an abundance of energy. It circulates around you and then becomes magnetic, attracting your tribe, the right team, the right clients, the right network of referral partners, whatever it is that you're seeking. You become a magnet when you are clear.

ENTREPRENEUR ACTION, HOMEWORK:

Record your Why video.

Now, you don't have to get all dressed up. You don't have to script it in advance. You don't have to share it with anybody. I just want you to pull out your smartphone or other video recording device, sit still, take a few deep breaths, and really connect with your Why.

Next, I want you to hit record and fully express your Why in a video, just for you. Think of it as an act of self-trust and self-love. Save it for your own personal records on your desktop, where you can easily reference it any time you're feeling discouraged or stuck.

It can be 30 seconds or 30 minutes. Sometimes, you'll be really surprised at what comes out of you when you start to record in a safe space. In 2022, I sat down and recorded a very impromptu video that documented the full story of my life. I thought it would take maybe 45-60 minutes, but I ended up talking for 3.5 hours, and it was the most freeing and loving thing I'd done for myself in a long time.

So, just like with everything else, go with the flow.

If you're energized by this experience, you can re-record it into something that's a little bit more thorough and professional to publish online, but I don't want you to start there because otherwise, you'll never do it!

I guarantee this is going to be a game-changer for you and your business.

TEAM ACTION LIST:

1. Ask your leader for their final Why statement(s) to add to your Workbook to memorialize it.

2. Use the Why statement(s) as an additional accountability tool company-wide.

   - For example, if you were on my team and saw my Why statements, that could serve as an indicator to you that when I'm stuck in a decision, you could suggest I tune in and see what my Intuition is guiding me to do. If you were to see me wrestling with what content to write on social media, you could suggest I share my voice authentically. As a member of my team, you could proactively find ways to recognize my efforts so I felt seen, or you could vocalize your appreciation for something specific I said so I felt heard.

   - It's not manipulation when you openly and genuinely share. To help fill someone's unmet need is an act of care and service. It's just that most people haven't been exposed to The Work to even know what their unmet needs are. That's why I pray for everyone's support in sharing this book with others. There is so much Impact to be made.

3. Encourage your leader to make a Why video they feel comfortable sharing online so prospective community members can meaningfully connect with your brand (which will activate word of mouth).

4. Have a company-wide quarterly meeting to review your Why statement(s) and openly address any areas for improvement both internally as a team, and externally with clients, community, and strategic partners.

You are now ready to move into the final pillar of the Foundational Four Framework. This is a call to action to revisit and redefine your Values more deeply than you might have considered before so you have unwavering conviction in your boundaries to then attract the right, qualified individuals into your tribe.

You are making BIG strides and are nearly through the steps to get and stay in Alignment.

"Don't ask yourself what the world needs.
Ask yourself what makes you come alive
and then go do that.

Because what the world needs
is people who have come alive."
- Howard Thurman

> ## I'm Doing The Work!
>
> If you haven't yet emailed me at amber@infiniteimpactbook.com with the subject line "I'M DOING THE WORK" I hope you'll do so now. But this time, tell me you just locked in your Why statement(s). I'd be delighted if you would share your Why with me. I really want to celebrate you and your courage!

CHAPTER 8

VALUES

Early in March 2020, I rushed downstairs to grab coffee before my first client call of the day. I stopped in my tracks when I heard the news that the world was about to change in a very significant way. It was time to prepare.

I cleared time in my schedule and held an emergency team meeting. I let the team know what was coming—that they may hear about other companies laying employees off—and I wanted to be very clear that they were safe. I had weathered economic storms before. I show up with strength in crisis and fiercely protect my family (which is how I feel about my team).

Two days later, mass hysteria started to break out. We reassured clients and became the voice of calm in our online platform. I had my regularly scheduled Friday morning call with my mentor and told him, "Ken, I have an idea."

I hesitated. If I said it out loud, I knew I'd have to hold myself accountable and follow through on the idea. That's just who I am. I lean in, face my fears, and follow through. But I was scared. Ironically, I wasn't afraid of COVID, or for the company, or revenue, or anything like that. I was afraid to be seen and heard. I've always felt I was capable of significance, but there had been a strong dose of resistance to burying that belief. I wasn't sure I had the energy, on top of running a team of 18 and being a present mother to a toddler, to step into the idea with unwavering excellence.

Ken was very familiar with the look on my face and nudged me forward.

I continued. "People are hurting and in such fear right now…I think I need to run a two-week live-streaming event to help. I could invite 30 or 40 of my peers—speakers, authors, and thought leaders—to have conversations about how to cope both personally and professionally at this time. There would be no sales pitch and no opt-in offers. We would just offer targeted business advice, facilitate meaningful discussion and connection, and help elevate us all out of this economic state in a high-integrity, high-Impact way. I could call it *The Elevate Series*."

It just spilled out. The idea had come to me that morning, and I wasn't even sure what I had just shared with him. It felt like it had been downloaded through my intuition.

No sooner did I finish blurting out the concept than I immediately put my hands over my face in hiding. *I didn't wanna.* Resistance was coming up in me BIG time. Who did I think I was coming up with an idea like this? I didn't want to be seen on a large scale. *What if I embarrassed myself in front of these well-respected speakers? What if it really was a dumb idea?* I wasn't ready. (Ken and *so many others* would have disagreed. Isn't it crazy how we battle with ourselves in these ways??)

He vocalized what I already sensed in that moment. I had to do it.

I rallied the team that afternoon, and invites to potential speakers went out the same day. I designed the graphics, wrote the promo emails, coded all web pages, built the speaker onboarding, and created the full virtual event series infrastructure over the weekend. Monday at 1 pm, I went live on all social platforms for the kick-off stream of *The Elevate Series*.

I followed through on the calling, but not without a great deal of emotional baggage hidden beneath the surface. There was no Foundational Four Framework to reference back then. I hadn't innovated The Work yet. My buried belief about being seen and using my voice was flaring up. I breathed through the discomfort and focused my mind on being in service.

I dared to step out onto that virtual global stage (at a time when everyone was glued to their apps) to vocalize my beliefs about connection, moving through fear, and supporting one another. The response was overwhelming in all the best ways. We had incredible reach and volumes of comments, emails, and DMs, all sharing gratitude. The speakers, some of the top in the country at that time, praised my leadership (which I secretly deflected since I've always been afraid of growing an ego after witnessing it in others).

<u>I felt liberated for daring to listen to my intuition and allowing myself to be fully self-expressed at the kick-off!</u> And a few days later…I lost my voice. Laryngitis. (You can't even make this stuff up.)

I resorted to asking two of the speakers if they could take over hosting the next full week of my live-stream series (eleven scheduled 45-minute interviews). I'm so thankful to Heather Hubbard and Hal Runkel for their belief in me and support of the series.

Rather than hiding in disappointment, I doubled down on what I could **give**. Choosing to stay in service offered me inner freedom and playfulness. As I attended each discussion, instead of talking, I held up post-it notes with my comments (it got a big laugh and created more connection!), carried a huge smile on my face, and offered my high-energy enthusiasm through the screen. It was perfect.

The Elevate Series ended up being a significant turning point in my career. After it ended, I was immediately offered nearly two dozen speaking engagements, my client roster exploded, and it was time to grow the organization. We grew by 80% that year, and more than 70% the following year, achieving the prestigious Inc. 5000 award as being one of the fastest-growing companies in America.

And…I was out of Alignment and didn't know it at the time.

I knew my macro-Vision and Avatar with deep clarity. I knew how to powerfully operate in marketing, customer journey, growing sales, and fulfilling my service offerings. My confidence was high.

Where I fell short was in my micro-Vision, my Why, and my Values. Plus, I hadn't yet created the Course-Correction exercise that was needed to help me overcome my resistance.

I'd doubled down on what I was confident in and yet had no awareness of the threat ahead that came from not being fully in Alignment as my opportunity for Impact hit.

As my company started to grow, I gave away my power (leadership) to new team leaders I perceived knew better than me. After all, I hadn't run a company that size before.

In fact, I had no formal business training beyond the excellent sales rep and management training I received in my years selling Cutco Cutlery. (You'll learn the whole story in Chapter 10.)

I've had such a successful career because I deeply care about each person I interact with. I have a pure heart for service. I am well-researched. I'm also unwavering in my follow-through out of fear of letting someone down. These are all valuable personality traits I cultivated out of the most painful experiences of my past. Nature teaches us that beauty and ugliness (yin and yang) co-exist simultaneously. Despite all I was doing right, it was not enough to overcome my incongruence.

In May of 2020, a very successful businessman named Darius booked a meeting with me. He was referred by a past client and needed support to launch his book on core values.

On the call, he asked if I had company Core Values. "I do! Let me look them up in my Google Drive, one sec," I responded. He laughed and passionately shared that mine was a common response to that question, and he was on a mission to get other businesses to see the value and importance of living their values. That means knowing them so well that they become the language of the organization, as well as the accountability and decision-making tool that releases pressure from the CEO. Releasing pressure sounded really nice to me at that moment. I had to experience what he was talking about.

In looking at our official Core Values before I met Darius ("official" because I had a graphic of them that I posted on social media one day, lol…), they were:

- Connection
- Open and Honest Communication
- Commitment to Excellent Service
- Growth

I was proud of them. I just couldn't remember them—and I certainly wasn't using them as an accountability tool—which meant I needed to go deeper.

Over the next six months, we launched Darius' book and he coached my team through his process for defining and rolling out our Core Values, not just internally, but also in our marketing and sales—everywhere.

Here's where we collectively landed:

> **Meaningful Connection** - We elevate every experience with warm smiles and open hearts. People light up when they are around us because they feel seen, heard, understood, and appreciated. We are fully open, present, and engaged. We intentionally go deeper in key relationships by having authentic and honest conversations. We are honest with ourselves and others in a way that shows grace, compassion, and humility. We speak the truth, in kindness, even when it's not easy.
>
> **Unwavering Excellence** - We are obsessed with a consistently superior quality of experience, product, and relationship. This means owning our mistakes, learning from them, and closing any open loops. We are committed to giving our best in every situation, especially when it's hard.
>
> **Better Together** - We use our unique gifts and complementary strengths to amplify our collective impact. We assume good intentions in our conversations, check our egos at the door, and put others before ourselves. We are purposeful about recognizing and actively appreciating the work of those around us. We value the co-creation process and explore ideas from multiple angles.

Lean In - We are courageous in exploring new ideas and processes that challenge the status quo. We actively learn from leaders both inside and outside the industry to adapt and grow. We have a culture of ideation and innovation and are always seeking the best path forward as a team.

Deeply Fulfilled - We help people do something they love that makes a difference in the world and take immense pride in the quality and impact of our work. People come to us to pursue the deepest feelings of self-actualization. We challenge and encourage them to grow into their best self. We celebrate our shared values and unique perspectives while creating a culture of acceptance and belonging.

This was an absolute game-changer for us during that high-growth phase and continues to be a sacred way of operating as we move forward.

Here are some ways our Values help us day-to-day:

- In our marketing, we embed the language of the Values into our social posts, videos, newsletters, opt-in pages, pricing menu, and more. They exist everywhere because they are innately us. It's our way of being. Prospects see those Values and either connect to them or not, creating a baked-in qualification process.
    - (There is a deeper psychology behind this, which we will explore in Chapters 10 and 11. Your approach to marketing will never be the same!)
- If a team member starts underperforming, we immediately evaluate their degree of upholding the Values to pinpoint where support is needed. If the behavior continues, we hold a meeting where they openly discuss the Values as the accountability manager (not me).

- For example, if I tell a team member, "You're not doing a good enough job, what's up?" that's very different from saying, "As you know, one of our Core Values is Unwavering Excellence. How do you feel you are performing in relation to that Value, and what can we do together to support you in adopting that more fully?" We move out of an attacking, high-emotion experience into a more supportive environment that has serious accountability attached to it. We write up a performance improvement plan and work to save the team member. In cases where they don't turn things around, I feel more clear and empowered in the process of transitioning that team member out instead of feeling extremely guilty when letting them go (which is how I used to feel).
- We review our Values when making key business decisions, such as whether or not to put on an event, accept speaking invitations for certain communities, let go of a client who is creating conflict, promote products or services, and so on. Each question we ask refines our business model into something that is more and more congruent with who we are and how we want to experience life as a whole.
    - This very process helped me make some of the scariest decisions of my life. One included scaling down from a team of 37 to a team of 7 in just under two years. It was important to me to carry the extreme weight of this decision, to significantly delay meeting my own needs so that I could be responsible, caring, and supportive to others during the transition as much as I was humanly capable of at the time.

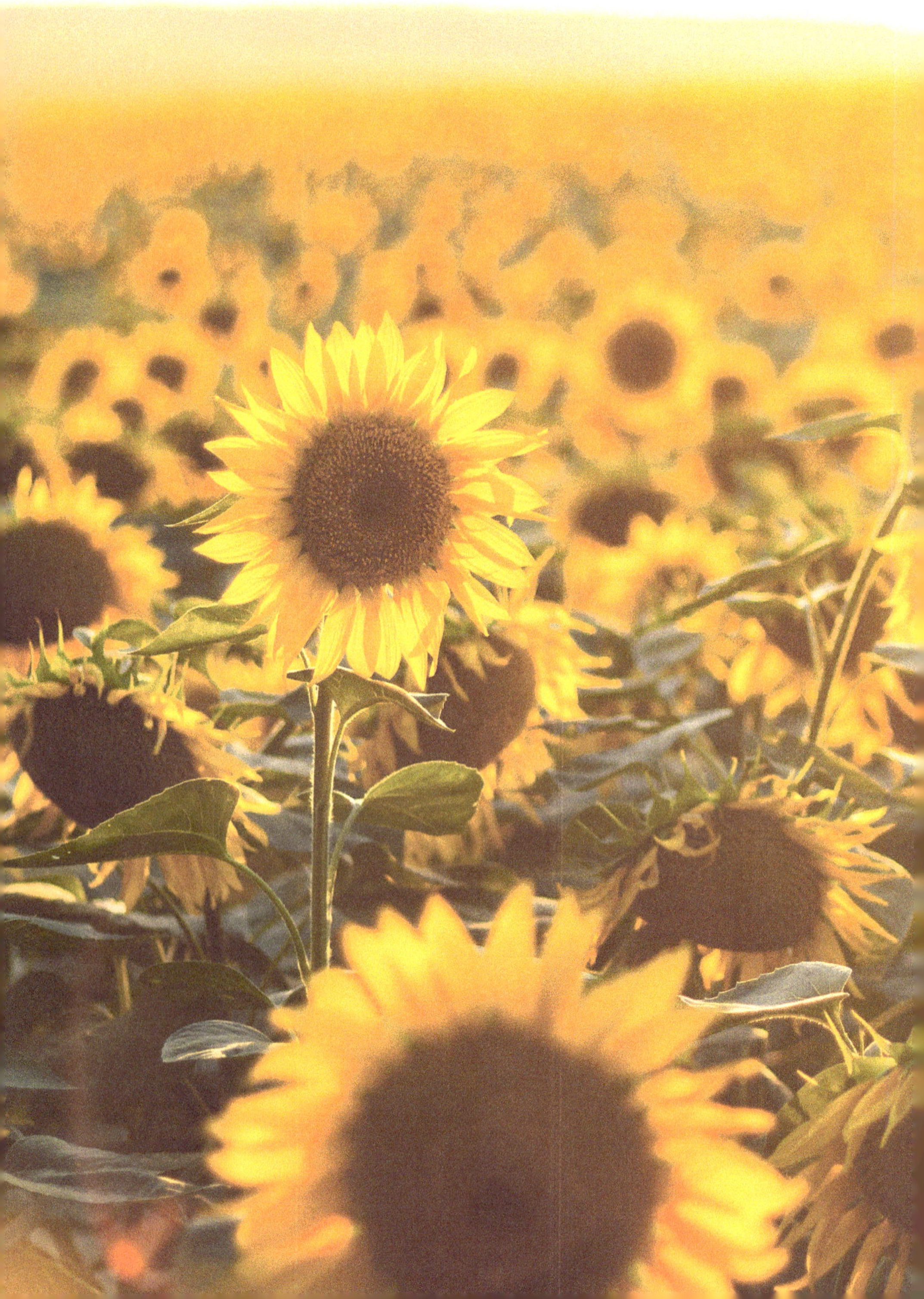

CORE VALUES EXERCISE

My personal Core Values do match my company Values. That's not always the case for people who do The Work. I have separate family Values that help drive co-parenting decisions and also ensure my son's dad and I treat each other with the utmost respect and care.

ENTREPRENEUR ACTION, HOMEWORK:

Consider the areas of your life where this tool might best serve you.

We'll now work through a light exercise to help you define or redefine your Values. There are numerous resources you can utilize to go deeper into this work should you so choose. For now, I'll walk you through the process that worked best for me:

ENTREPRENEUR ACTION, STEP 1:

Pull out a piece of paper, open a new tablet screen, or clear space on a whiteboard. I strongly encourage you to write during this exercise instead of typing. Write down every word you can think of that represents what you deeply care about.

Writing prompts:

- ☐ What happened recently that brought you increased joy, laughter, pride or love? Who were you with, and what did they do? If you were alone, what action, thought, or feeling took place?

- ☐ Consider all of the different roles you play in life, from leader or team member to parent or child, to spouse or friend, and so on.
- ☐ Look at what you appreciate about yourself. Perhaps it's paying team members or service providers on time, arriving early for meetings, attending all of your child's sports activities, or leaving love notes for people you care about. Then, pick a word that describes each act.
- ☐ What do you admire in other people? What do you cherish in how others operate?
- ☐ Think back in previous chapters to some of the experiences you had and beliefs you hold.
- ☐ What do you want to invite more of into your life?

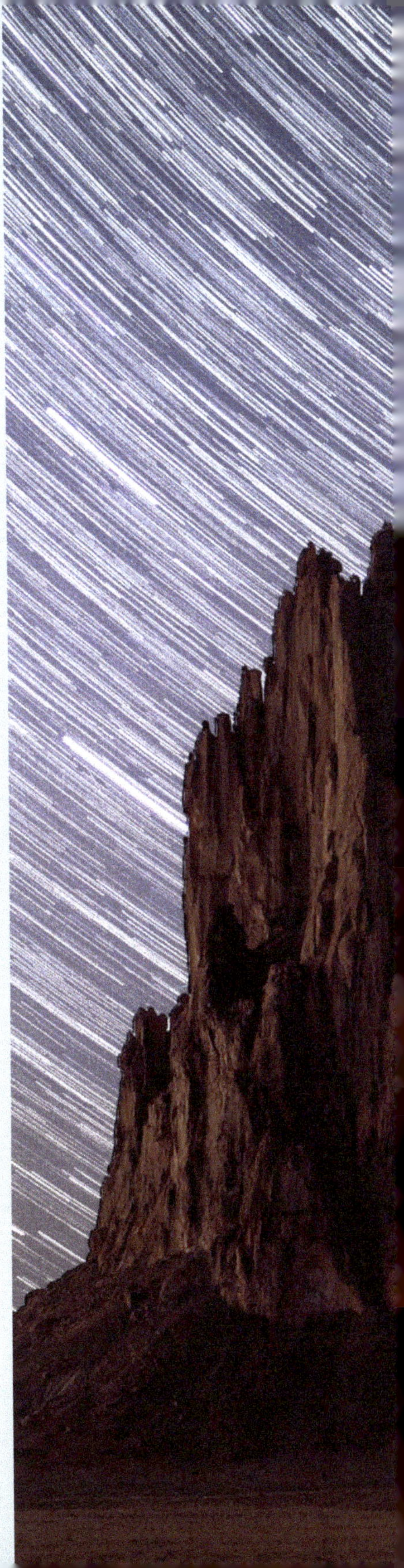

Troubleshooting:

1. Don't pause to consider each word, or edit yourself. Free-flow words that come to you until you find a natural stopping point. (For context, I initially wrote down roughly 60 words. Included were words like love, honesty, organization, healthy eating, kindness, respect, integrity, courage, play, adventure, and so on.)

2. Review past love notes, testimonials, or positive comments on your social channels. Looking at feedback people have given to you previously can help point you to what you value in yourself.

3. You can research "Core Value examples" or "Core Values lists" to look for prompts.

4. <u>Caution: Be careful of the trap of writing words that you see commonly, words that you think other people value, or what</u>

<u>you wish you valued</u>. The key is to pay attention to what really matters most deeply to you.

ENTREPRENEUR ACTION, STEP 2:

Organize your list and narrow it down to your 10 most important Values.

(What worked for me: I reviewed my full list and crossed out words that didn't grab me as much as others and circled the words that carried a high charge for me. I more deeply considered words that were similar—such as organized and efficient—to explore the difference between the two, and then I kept the one that mattered more to me.)

ENTREPRENEUR ACTION, STEP 3:

Refine your 10 Values into a Top 5. Then, do some wordplay to create specificity and evoke more resonance and creativity.

Not gonna lie…this step was much more difficult than the previous ones, and I needed help. I got as far as I could, then enlisted help from someone I highly regard who knows me really well. He helped me go deeper, and then Darius helped challenge the list, the team weighed in, and together we polished our list of Core Values.

There are varying opinions as to whether the CEO should come up with the Values alone, or if the team and/or others should get involved. I've seen each approach work out successfully. My opinion is:

Go your own way and do what is right for you.

If it wouldn't be disruptive, I would print that on every single page of this book because it's one of the most significant learnings you can walk away with.

As long as you **do** The Work, it matters less how you arrive at the answers. My wish for you is that you challenge yourself to go deeper and deeper. You'll learn so much about yourself, and it will be so rewarding in the end.

TEAM ACTION LIST:

1. I highly recommend that you work through this exercise to define your own personal Core Values before you collaborate with your leader on the company Values. Please share your Values with your leader so they can get to know you better and support meeting your needs.

2. Schedule a team meeting with your leader and see what came up for them in this exercise. If they would find it helpful, lean in and collaborate on the process of creating the company Values, then clearly itemize your final company Core Values in your workbook.

3. Consider if additional books, resources, or consulting would be helpful. The most important thing is that the leader trusts themselves to decipher their Values, define them, and use them as the language of the organization moving forward. If there is one person in the organization who needs to be 100% congruent with the Values, it's the business owner.

4. Discuss the option of creating a company Core Values video that can be displayed on your website, YouTube, and social channels. (See your Toolkit for an example.)

5. As the company grows, you'll want to ideate ways to integrate your Values into your meeting agendas, proposals, employee reviews, job descriptions, and more.

Looking back on that time in my career in 2020, I see with clarity that the Values were inside of me all along. I just had to go through the process of finding and defining them.

During *The Elevate Series*, I dared to move through my fears (lean in), I wanted a group of Impact-driven professionals to collaborate with (better together), I had the vision to facilitate meaningful discussion (meaningful connection), I did everything I could think of to offer an excellent experience for all (unwavering excellence), and after it was complete I was definitely deeply fulfilled.

> "Your beliefs become your thoughts,
> your thoughts become your words,
> your words become your actions,
> your actions become your habits,
> your habits become your values, and
> your values become your destiny."
> - Mahatma Gandhi

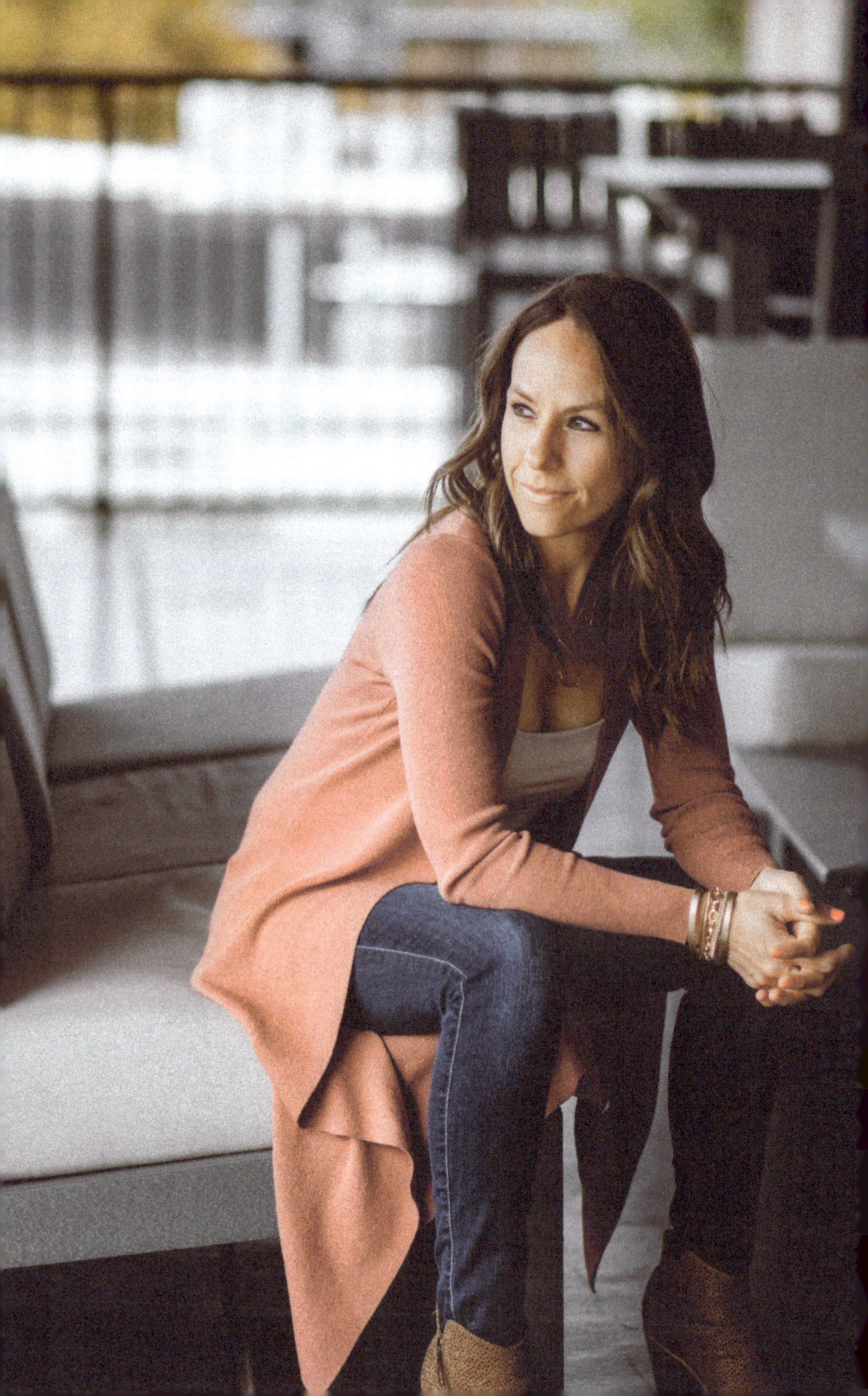

PART THREE

BOOKS & BUSINESS OPTIMIZATION

CHAPTER 9

BOOKS

*"If you can dream it, you can do it
The way to get started is to quit talking
and begin doing."
- Walt Disney*

In the early days, before the really big BOOM of online business, the internet was the great frontier. It was so fun to write a blog post and watch it get ranked in a #1 search results spot in Google overnight. In comparison to the chaos internet marketing has become today, growing an online business back then was a walk in the park. Your task was to consistently put out great content, period.

In the 2010s, social media in combination with ads and funnels brands changed the online landscape forever. I observed the rise of the "sexy marketing headline" that would promise you the sun, moon, and stars when you order a $27 tripwire. But hurry, this offer is disappearing, and your life will be in ruins if you don't act now…

On call after call with prospects, I'd listen to entrepreneurs who were nearly out of money and were running out of time. They had invested ten thousand, fifty thousand, one hundred thousand dollars…on courses and programs and/or ad agencies that didn't deliver on their promise. A dear friend shared he was $80,000 in the hole, stressed to the max, and afraid to tell his wife what had happened to their savings. I'd listen to stories about agencies that didn't do the work and wouldn't give refunds, freelancers who were paid up front and disappeared in the night, and coaches who were unreliable and unhelpful in their approach. Call after call, my heart got heavier and heavier.

I *knew* the value of the dollar by learning the hard way (…just like everything else I learned). I knew what it felt like to stand in line at the grocery store praying you had enough money on the card to avoid the embarrassment of putting items back. I knew the stress of counting every single dollar, feeling defeated after working so hard, and hoping to have enough money to pay my bills each month.

To hear *good-hearted people* share their private financial burdens with me after being duped by "experts" in my industry made me sick to my stomach. That darn headline promising the magic bullet blasted us into further mistrust with one another. I was struck with a gnawing in my gut to urgently find additional ways to help. Building websites that convert wasn't enough.

After hundreds of these calls, where the unhealed trauma and unmet needs from my childhood were being continually exposed (and quickly shoved back down again before anyone could see them), enough was finally enough. Frustration and rage seemed to grow inside of me overnight like a magic beanstalk, as I replayed memories of being duped, gaslit, and abandoned.

I turned those feelings into the jet fuel needed to spend long days tirelessly helping good people do good work in the world. I didn't just want the "good ones" to win—I needed them to win—and a new chapter in my life was born.

This awakening became the birth of my obsession to help entrepreneurs grow profitable and impactful online businesses.

First, I innovated **Leverage To Scale**, a revolutionary training program that would teach a marketing freelancer on your team how to do your marketing for you. This saved entrepreneurs around the world *many tens of thousands of dollars* from hiring agencies. It kept the operation running inside their company so if a team member exited, a new person could take over and pick up right where they last left off, further protecting the business owner.

This program made a significant dent but still wasn't enough to combat the volume of failed businesses that stood for important change. There was more to be done. The rise of the "influencer" was growing exponentially, while I observed humanity getting more disconnected and individuals more isolated.

In the months leading up to 2020, I found myself on more calls with authors, speakers, and coaches who were taking their final breaths of belief that their lives could have significant meaning. They weren't just on the verge of giving up on their cause and business, I could feel them on the verge of giving up on themselves, and giving up on the belief that they could create a real Impact. My spirits started to dim. I was growing more and more ashamed of an industry I had helped shape.

That's when, in the winter of 2019, my mentor Ken asked me why I was so busy. I'd worked myself into a frenzy trying to help as many people as I could and felt proud to have such a meaningful purpose. Loved ones around me didn't quite see it the same way as the hours passed by, taking me away from family time. I tried to find solace in knowing I was doing my very best every day to balance purpose and all my passions, but most days ended in defeat, feeling that my best simply wasn't enough.

With COVID's global crisis came a deafening wake-up call from the auto-pilot, desensitized fog we'd been living in. The market shifted dramatically. Individuals were in such a state of mistrust that they weren't so easily duped by promising ads, funnels, and offers. They paused to take time to do more due diligence and ensure they were clear on what they were buying. *I was SO excited to see people waking up to their values!*

With that wake-up came a surge of individuals writing books to help others, and I was ready for them.

Authors booked calls with me to inquire about the launch process. Their learning curve was steep, so it became my job to simplify the journey for them the best I could (otherwise, I knew they would never keep going—it would prove too difficult).

If you want to have a true Impact, you can't just slap up a brochure website, do a minimum amount of social media, launch quickly, and hope for the best (only to sell a few hundred copies). That story has been told too many times. ==We must change the narrative.==

These are the common mistakes most authors make:

- Not giving themselves enough runway (time) to market and launch.
- Not willing to go "all in."
- Not having a powerful plan that is rooted in proven marketing methodologies.
- Not setting aside a big enough budget for their marketing and book launch.
- Not delegating day-to-day operations to someone else, which sacrifices precious time they could spend doing the things only they can do.
- Not treating their book as a product that can (and should) be leveraged to create a seven-figure business.

In general, I recommend you have a healthy six-month planning and marketing runway before your book release date if you are self-publishing or using a hybrid publisher. However, if you are getting traditionally published, I typically like to suggest a 12-month runway. (If you don't know your publishing options, you'll want to ask questions in our Books & Business membership, or find a publishing production expert to consult with.)

The general rule is that it's never too early to start a strategic planning conversation to maximize your Impact. Ideally, you would start these conversations while you're in the early stages of *writing* the book so we can implement a marketing strategy into your chapters. A Books & Business strategist can design a powerful strategic plan that helps you monetize in advance of the launch to give you a bigger budget to reinvest into the amplification of your cause.

Once we solve that, some of the remaining hurdles many authors face include:

- Concerns about added workload crashing into an already busy schedule as they pursue The Author's Hero's Journey.
- Not liking the idea of being an "influencer."
- Not enjoying social media.

I have a solution for that:

(1) As shown below, I provide a structure to whip the author's online brand into shape, then count down to the book's release date with a logical and highly leveraged approach. I cut the fat everywhere I can.

(2) It's time to redefine what it means to be an influencer. To me, it's simply, "A leader who wants to positively Impact individuals who will then create further Impact in the world."

(3) I delegate the maximum amount of work to the author's team to protect their time and energy.

My **Leverage To Scale** marketing training program has been a consistent bestseller for many years because it got the marketing monkey OFF the entrepreneur's back. I expanded on that concept and next created a **Bestseller Book Launch Blueprint** course. This is another top-selling program that teaches a CMA and author how to launch a book and make it #1 on Amazon on their own, *saving them tens of thousands of dollars* on hiring outside help. Plus, they can reuse the program for all future launches. Both of these, as well as additional programs, are housed in my **NGNG Academy.**

I simply recommend that you:

1. Do The Work.

2. Collaborate with a *Books & Business strategist* to give you a target and roadmap.

3. Get your team trained (even if it's just one person) and let them execute the tasks necessary to grow your following.

4. Stay Aligned and harness your energy toward activities that grow your passion while simultaneously growing your following and authority, such as getting interviewed, speaking, working with customers, and writing.

5. ENJOY the process of growing your Infinite Impact.

Can I get you to agree to those steps?

What I love about book launches is that it's the PERFECT TIME to accomplish all of this work in one fell swoop.

6 PHASES OF A BOOK LAUNCH

My team and I guide authors through these phases to have a successful launch:

1. **PLATFORM:**

    a. We start by doing The Work to get you in Alignment and ready for Impact.

    b. We apply that to your branding so your Avatar feels an emotional connection to your brand and cause.

    c. We express that brand through a deeply strategic website that is anchored in a thoughtful and optimized customer journey that repeatedly and steadily converts qualified prospects into raving customers.

    d. I help train a CMA to do your marketing for you, including video optimization, social media, blog posts and SEO, email marketing, and metrics tracking using the *Leverage to Scale* training program.

    e. **Your role** in this phase is to stay Aligned, write the content only you can write, and record video in batches once per quarter (speaking to your Avatar to grow a meaningful connection). Not bad, eh?

2. **GROWTH:**

    a. Your brand, website, and foundational content marketing are finally working in harmony. Now it's time to grow your audience. The strategy for this must be thoughtfully customized to match your natural energy and passion. We commonly start with things like…

        i. Getting you interviewed on podcasts. There is absolutely a proper strategy for this activity that can organically unlock sales, referrals to more shows, and speaking opportunities.

        ii. Collaborating with other community leaders to co-host live stream discussions, facilitate workshops, and run virtual or in-person summits.

    b. This is also the time when we have a strong focus on growing revenue because, without that, I know you're more likely to self-sabotage out of fear your efforts won't pan out. This set of strategies must be thoughtfully customized, as well.

    c. **Your role** in this phase is to speak, network, and sell in an Aligned and natural way.

3. **RELATIONSHIP MANAGEMENT (RM):**

    a. This is an NGNG exclusive 3-4 month campaign designed to revive your existing network (including people you met years ago), reintroduce yourself and share your cause, lean in where there is interest in collaboration, and move forward with the individuals who are aligned and excited to help you promote your launch. **This is *the core strategy* of any book launch I orchestrate and is also available as a training program for teams in the NGNG Academy.**

i. John Lee Dumas was able to secure more than 10,000 pre-orders in 2.5 months using this one strategy. Amy Lafko was able to 7x her revenue post-launch after deploying this strategy. It is designed to offer you a naturally harmonious (and profitable!) outcome because it's anchored in creating human connection around a cause. By valuing each collaborative partner, they rise and shine to support because it feels good (mutual reciprocation).

b. **Your role** in this phase is to have meaningful conversations with folks and participate in collaboration that amplifies your Impact.

4. **TWO-MONTH COUNTDOWN:**

    a. At this stage, your entire platform is functioning harmoniously, and you're enjoying speaking (sharing your cause and ideas) and growing your audience.

    b. Your team will activate a specific sequence of weekly emails to your community and post social media content designed to prepare your audience to participate in the launch of your book (buy your book and help promote it).

    c. This is also when we ensure your book sales page is live and shining brightly, offering bonus content as a companion to the book (a way for you to capture email addresses and grow your audience even more!).

    d. **Your role** in this phase is only to stay consistent with your contribution as already stated above.

5. **<u>LAUNCH</u>:**

    a. <u>Authors who have done The Work</u> to stay in Alignment, and approach their launch week with pride, enjoyment, and readiness for Impact.

        i. Conversely, the average author who doesn't have this training walks into their launch week experiencing an array of heavy emotions tied to unworthiness and hiding has a very chaotic schedule and is micro-managing to distract themselves. This is what I've worked so hard to prevent.

    b. There are several tactical tasks that must be done to confirm readiness such as testing your bonus opt-in form, selecting Amazon categories, sending reminders to promoters, and more. (You are highly supported in the digital Toolkit companion to this book found at InfiniteImpactBook.com.)

    c. **Your role** in this phase is to focus more on your well-being practice than normal. Get plenty of rest, remind yourself of your progress, focus on gratitude for all of the people showing up in support of you, remind yourself of your Vision and Why, etc.

6. **<u>SCALE</u>:**

    a. Platform, Growth, and Relationship Management activities continue long-term. **<u>The longer you stay in Alignment and consistent in your actions, the faster your following, revenue, and Impact will grow.</u>** It's truly that simple.

Transactionally incentivizing people to take action and spamming communities are not strategies I recommend to my clients because they tend to do more harm than good. In fact, it's that very approach that has contributed to our dread toward marketing to begin with.

Instead, I focus my work with authors on a more collaborative approach rooted in creating meaningful connection with people who believe in their message. Meaning, I put operations in place and teach them how to create win-wins with colleagues, peers, and fans who believe in the same cause.

When you Align with others who share a similar Vision and Values set, they can't help but be compelled to help you.

That's very different than them feeling forced or incentivized to help you. Remember, I'm advocating for a more natural and meaningful approach to growth. The days of forcing are soon to be behind you.

It was this dedication, team innovation, and *hard, hard work* over many years that grew NGNG's Impact. We achieved the Inc. 5000 award for being one of the fastest-growing advertising companies in America (an incredibly competitive category in a hugely competitive award program!). I had been so head-down doing my job to make a difference that I was a little stunned when the award notice came in. My family and team celebrated more than I did—to me, it was a mark of Impact, and I just knew I wanted to keep going.

The drive to help others feel seen, heard, and valued was, and still is, insatiable. Embedding my Vision into each client's strategy, building operations for their team to execute, and then watching the Impact unfold naturally was a thrill, to say the least. My Vision is being actualized, causing a ripple effect beyond what I can calculate. Infinite Impact is happening in real-time all around the planet. This is what awaits you.

There is something about seeing another person light up right in front of your eyes. If you are fully present and attentive to the person in front of you, you can see the exact moment they feel seen. Their eyes shift in focus, the corners of their mouth raise, their back sits a little straighter, and hope has landed in their body. It's magical…and yet *so simple* to achieve.

It can happen the moment someone lands in your virtual meeting room, asking how you are. In that moment you have an important choice. You can passively say, "Good, you?" or you can take a beat, consider how you are, and answer genuinely, "I'm good! I feel grateful, hopeful, and focused forward. How about yourself?" or "I'm a little challenged by a few things, but that means I'm having a character-building day and it's only going to help me be better moving forward, you?" It's little moments of connection like this that can change a person's trajectory.

A 10-year-old boy named Caiden (my son's best friend's older brother) recently told his mom that he liked coming over to my house. She asked why. His response was, "She makes me feel seen."

This was a moment in time I was guided to after the pain of my past by listening to my intuition and being led by my Values. I arrived at the moment where my Vision was yet again achieved and where, in return, my Why was satisfied. He felt seen, and in an instant, so did I. Mutual reciprocation. My heart was healing, my body filled with a surge of energy, and I felt fully alive.

Caiden and I had a meaningful conversation where I raved about how important it is for him to carry the torch and help others feel seen. The feeling of Impact in that moment was palpable. Like the Butterfly Effect…it felt like the future was adjusted once more.

My cause—meaningful connection—is so important that it guides every strategy I create for a book launch or business growth. It's infused in SOPs I write for clients, and training videos I make for their team.

I'll never stop innovating ways to guide more people back to trust and meaningful connection.

What matters at the end of the day is how we make people feel. That in turn shapes how we feel. Mutual reciprocation is the name of the game.

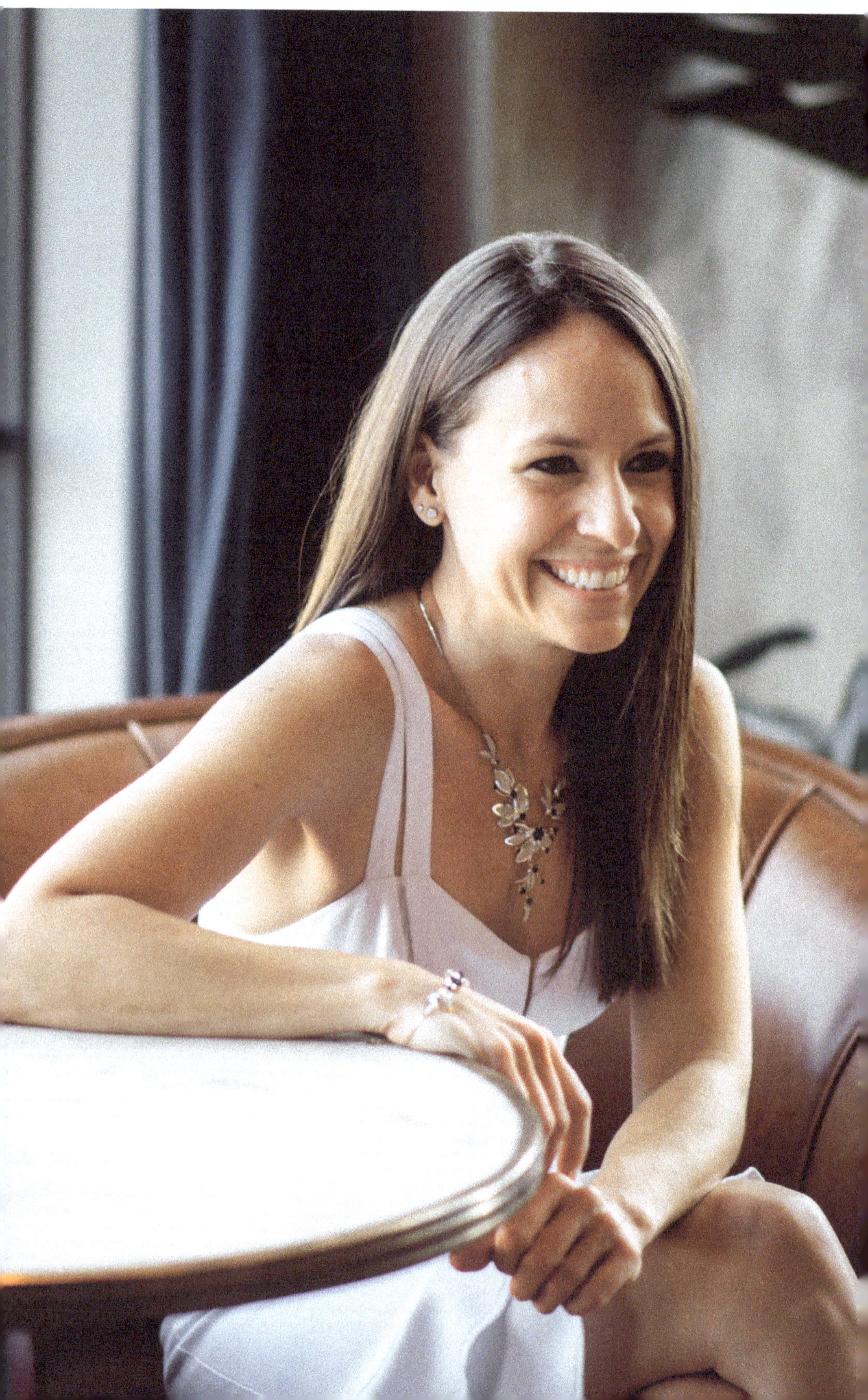

CHAPTER 10

BUSINESS

"Do not go where the path may lead, go instead where there is no path and leave a trail."
- Ralph Waldo Emerson

In 2007, when my company was founded, I had no formal business strategy.

In the few years prior, my entrepreneurial spirit was alive and kicking as a Division Sales Manager for Cutco Cutlery. Working 100-hour weeks recruiting, training, and speaking was the norm in the summertime, but my spirit was alive. I was challenged, celebrated, and rewarded…I was happy. Heavy feelings from the past of being misunderstood, rejected, and lost were melting off my conscious thought patterns. I was finally experiencing the feeling of freedom I'd longed for.

And, I knew deep down there was more in store for me in life. I had to know what it was.

I put in almost a year's worth of notice, trained up my replacement, and took to the proverbial open road. *(Isn't it amazing the risks we're willing to take when we're younger…it's time to bring more of that risk-taking into this, and future seasons of life, too…)*

In a gig that led to the long-term gig, I played the role of event planner for two local Denver conferences that taught entrepreneurs how to get cash capital into their businesses and how to market online. I had no clue what a blog was, or much about actual entrepreneurship other than the marketing, sales, and operations training I had at Cutco. The learning curve was steep, but I was having a blast. The web developer on staff, Marty, took me under his wing and taught me a lot about websites and internet marketing. The conferences were a catalyst for my deep dive into learning about website coding, AdWords, SEO, Copywriting, Funnels, and so much more. I was hooked (and didn't even have full awareness as to why). I just let the good times roll.

I put my self-taught SEO wisdom to good use and found that two of the most searched phrases in Google in 2007 were "insight" and "develop." That's when I decided InsightfulDevelopment.com would be the domain name for my new blog. I felt so clever.

In early Fall, a woman located in Canada contacted me through my website and asked if I could help her build and manage her guest blogging platform. I literally didn't know how to respond. I was just dabbling! Was I really ready for this? What would I even charge?! How would I even get this done?! My insecurity and fear bubbled up, but I let my curiosity win.

Around that same time, a woman who'd observed me event planning reached out and asked if she could teach me how to launch books so I could manage that service for the authors in her California publishing company. It felt like the Universe was conspiring (...and I was listening).

I did the brave thing and ultimately said yes to both. A friend suggested, "Hey Amber, you should probably file an LLC."

"What's that?" I replied. (That's just how naive I was.)

The next thing I knew, I was staring at a blinking cursor on the State of Colorado website, stumped by a line entry that asked for my company name. My internal dialogue was racing, "Company name...company name...I had no ambition to even start a company...company name?! Just put anything down, it doesn't matter, and no one will see it anyway...but what if someday it turns into something that matters? A name...A name..."

I let my intuition prevail and "**NGNG** Enterprises" (which stands for **No Guts No Glory!**) was born. I felt warm inside thinking of the times my mom would bend down and say that phrase to me when I was a little girl. I watched her have the courage to be a single mom, to turn down men's proposals, to sacrifice to put my sister and me in the best private school in town, to be one of the first Americans to hike a mountain range in Tibet, to host an event for the Dalai Lama, to nudge me out of the nest to spend two weeks in Italy when I was in 8th grade, to make great professional strides in a male-dominated industry, to lean into hard conversations, and to dare to be different than how she was raised. I wanted to model her bravery and be the best me I could be, too.

==NGNG became my mantra.==

And just like that, I became a business owner. With zero formal business education, I was forced to focus on the following non-negotiables to help me ride the wave past the 90% failure rate as a new business owner, and continue to lead the business forward into our second decade of Impact.

- → Always do what I say I'm going to do, no matter what. Follow-through and reliability were of the utmost importance. I stayed true to that principle through significant relationship changes, pregnancy challenges and loss, extreme insecurity, and mind-crunching challenges. I was determined to be the place where clients could find relief from so many other service providers who were less reliable.

- → No borrowing or overspending. Anything I spent was strictly out of my profit. I had learned this principle the hard way as a contractor for Cutco. I was a late bloomer in understanding the law regarding estimated taxes, and I found myself always behind on payments and racking up penalty fines for the first few years. I was unwilling to experience that pain again. Instead, I focused on saving and reinvesting back into the business to support its growth.

- → Respond fast, be loving, and produce excellence in design, copy, and overall service. I invested more time in projects than I was paid for in the early days. I showered each person in front of me with honest kindness and gratitude. I treated others the way I wanted to be treated. I ensured my best was always what people experienced.

- → Be consistent. My SEO research taught me the unwavering importance of staying consistent in marketing, and it was common sense to apply that to a client experience. I strengthened my young muscles of discipline and focus to produce weekly blogs, daily social posts, weekly newsletters, and prompt replies to client emails. One foot in front of the other, year after year.

BUSINESS OWNER EXERCISE

ENTREPRENEUR ACTION:

List the non-negotiables for your business.

Writing prompts:

- ☐ What kind of experience do YOU want to have in your business?
- ☐ How do you want your followers, prospects, and clients to feel?
- ☐ What kind of experience do you want your team to have?
- ☐ Consider your Core Values.
- ☐ Consider your mindset toward finances, communication, organization, customer service, leadership, relationships at large, and personal lifestyle goals.

_____

_____

_____

_____

_____

While I had no clue what a balance sheet was or how to create a formal business plan, I knew that I craved feeling seen, heard, and valued. That awareness guided some of my non-negotiables because I figured if I craved that, maybe others did too. By committing to lead with that, the rest came together naturally in time.

WHAT ALIGNMENT LOOKS LIKE IN SALES

In Chapter 5 we did The Work to define your Avatar, and in that chapter, I began by telling you about my meeting with good ol' Larry back in 2010. You remember, the restaurant paper product guy?

Well, I've thought about Larry consistently throughout my career because he played such an instrumental role in helping me get and stay in Alignment with sales.

<u>AmberV's View of Sales</u>: *Sales is an opportunity to "continue the conversation," to connect and serve. With the right fit, we'll move forward in collaboration toward a better outcome or experience.*

I was still so new in the business that I didn't have the knowledge yet to be in full company Alignment, but consistently growing cash flow gave me oxygen and time to learn the rest.

As you'll recall back then, I offered 60-minute discovery calls with anyone interested in working with me. I was closing about 25% of the time, which meant it would take me four hours of calls to secure a website client, not to mention the time in email communication and proposal creation. That simply wasn't sustainable. After Larry's call when I realized there had to be a better way, I picked myself up, dusted myself off, and started to analyze what was happening.

Here's what I learned:

- The Larrys of the world would come to my website and see I offered a service building websites.
- They would fill out a short contact form. I would receive the email inquiry.
- I'd reach out to Larry offering a time to get to know one another, explain my process, and answer any questions.
- A 60-minute call would be booked where I'd find out if a new client was onboarding.

I then stepped out of my business owner tendencies of "needing" an outcome to grow the business, and instead, looked at this experience from the lens of the prospect. Here's what I imagined their experience to be:

- I need a website. I found someone who builds websites.
- I fill out a contact form to request more information. I get an email saying I have to book a 60-minute call just to get the details I need to make a buying decision.
- I'll find out on the call if this person meets my needs, otherwise I'll have to start the search all over and hope for a better match next time.

Wow, right? The customer journey looks completely different from the customer's perspective. From my perspective it made sense to offer a call; however, I didn't consider that prospects may have felt I was hiding information, trapping them into a live call, making them jump through hoops, etc.

That is why it is *so important* to put yourself in someone else's shoes to ensure you're offering the best possible experience to others. When that happens, sales grow far more effortlessly. After seeing Larry's probable perspective, it was obvious to me what I needed to change.

Here's what I did to get into Alignment with my sales:

1. I slightly tweaked my website content to niche down.

    a. I said, "I build websites for authors, speakers, and coaches" (instead of "I build websites").

2. I created a 3-minute video that sat on the top of my home page.

    a. The video introduced me, explained what I do, who I do it for, went through the step-by-step process, and suggested the next action. (I now call this a "door-greeter video" and offer further training on this in your companion Toolkit.) The action was an invitation to download my pricing menu PDF.

    b. The prospect would give me their name and email address so I knew where to email the menu (effectively allowing me to capture the prospect's contact information so I could personally follow up).

3. As promised, an automated email was sent including the pricing menu.

    a. My pricing menu (which you can scope out and model today at ngngenterprises.com) was nearly 20 pages long, including full transparency about process and pricing, packed with testimonials and proof of my success.

    b. I set up a 5-email nurture sequence. I added a survey up front so I could get to know who was coming into my orbit, shared my personal story, more fully listed out our services, and ultimately continued to casually suggest that prospects book a call with me.

4. I offered a 30-minute call (down from 60 minutes) to answer any questions (instead of explaining the process and pricing).

As I shared at the start of this book, I embedded that "customer journey" into my website platform, and the results still astound me to this day:

→ **I cut my sales call time spent by 50%.**
> I saved time and energy by not having to repeat my process and payment options over and over on each call.

→ **My sales pitch anxiety disappeared.**
> The scary part of them asking for my rates and next steps was already revealed to them before the call.

→ **I saved significant time because 95% of prospects who scheduled a call became qualified buyers.**
> The people who aren't a fit self-select out instead of requesting a call.

→ **I improved my closing percentage from 25% to 60%+, which greatly grew my confidence.**
> My customers LOVE that I educate them up front and don't hide the information they want. No duping here.

→ **We doubled our profit.**
> By having consistency in the type of clients we onboarded, we greatly improved efficiency through repeatable operations.

→ **We more easily grew the size of our email following.**
(And with qualified subscribers…) All by asking people to "opt-in" in exchange for our pricing menu.

And the icing on the cake? Call after call, prospects would start by saying, "Amber! I feel like I already know you. I've seen your videos, and I felt like you were talking directly to me! I downloaded your pricing menu and already know what I want to order, but just have a few quick questions first…"

My response? "Hi! It's nice to meet you!"

I felt so free, proud of my progress, and excited for the future. (I still do!)

After nearly 20 years of strategic planning, I now have the vantage point to know you are likely a LOT closer to a great outcome than you think.

In my case, all I needed was a little more specificity in my content, a short video, a PDF, and a short opt-in nurture sequence. That's what it took to grow sales into the multiple six figures as a business owner with no formal business education!

For more than 15 years, I've not changed my customer journey or sales approach!

I let my Vision guide me and took the initiative to thoughtfully design an experience my Avatar would appreciate. I have an optimized customer journey that repeatedly and steadily converts qualified prospects into raving customers. I don't have to wonder where my next client is coming from. And that has been true through economic uncertainty and global crisis.

Here's what it can look like to be in Alignment with your sales:

- You attract, qualify, and sell based on your Values. You're not interested in working with an individual outside of that Values set because you know it will eventually lead to conflict, confusion, and temporary self-disempowerment.
- You're not stressed, wondering where your next sale will come from.
- You are repulsed by language like "tripwire" because you're here to change lives, not treat people like a number.
- You look carefully at your website most weeks to confirm you are representing yourself to others in the way you want (or make changes so you stay in Alignment). Since you are a human evolving, your platform must be always current and accurate.
- You don't feel like you're selling, you feel like you're helping.
- You're not focused on what you can get, you're focused on what you can give.
- You make the sales call all about being super present, asking good questions to find out what's really going on with your prospect (what they are afraid of, resistant to, need, want), listening extremely carefully, and allowing your intuition to guide your offer based on what they need most.
- You charge what you're worth because you believe in mutual reciprocation, in a fair exchange of value, in your self-worth, and in your ability to make a transformative change for your clients.
- You are specific, organized, and clear on your offer to eliminate confusion or buyer's remorse. You clearly articulate what you can do, how long it will take, and what customers will experience because you respect their time and your own.

My priority has never been to have the biggest email list or the largest social media follower count. Instead, it has always been to work with people in a mutually loving and respectful way, where we collaborate to get a lot of powerful work done in order to help more people in the world. I'd do that job ALL day long. I designed everything I ever wanted to experience in a sales and client capacity, and as a result, it NEVER felt like "selling" to me. It felt like a mature and professional exchange of value. As a result, word of mouth spread and became our #1 marketing strategy. This is the prize of being in Alignment.

Whereas my company offers started with branding and website design, I offered coaching to clients to help them with their customer journey and sales too. The rave reviews and case studies started pouring in. Speaking engagements and strategic partnerships followed.

I was hungry to learn more, implement this strategy myself to prove its effectiveness, and then offer more support to others. My inner geek was playing all out. I expanded into planning and building out infrastructure for almost every monetization offering you can think of, including webinars, membership sites, summits, courses, digital products, consulting packages, and more. The business continued to grow using the same customer journey and sales approach.

I dug deeper into the powers of online marketing and began strategizing in that area too. I'd proven the importance of blogging, SEO, and publishing valuable content consistently. Video was just starting to grow in mainstream popularity by the early 2010s. Of course, I already knew the power of video from the customer journey on my website and other uses, so it was natural for me to experiment with video in my marketing.

WHAT ALIGNMENT LOOKS LIKE IN MARKETING

AmberV's View of Marketing: Creating a connection, sharing your beliefs, and making an invitation.

One day in 2016, business was booming for my small team of 15 contractors. I was fully immersed in the stage of entrepreneurship where I was the center of every idea, decision, and approval. And at the time, I loved it. It met my need for a challenge, proving over and over I could get things done well. (This was before the big "wake up" where I needed to Course-Correct).

This particular summer day, when the long daylight hours allowed me to squeeze in an extra couple of hours of work with a little less guilt, I was feeling the pressure to get my weekly marketing activities done.

I looked at a piece of paper to my right, which held the names of all my clients who were expecting work to be delivered the next day. I looked at my computer screen in front of me. The blinking cursor was holding me accountable at the end of a blog post I'd just spent 35 minutes writing. I clicked publish and moved on to my final marketing activity of the week—that dang email newsletter that needed to be prepared and sent. Fifty minutes later, I scheduled the email to send to my community in the morning. The sun was setting and the clock offered me no solace, just more guilt and pressure.

Once again, I put my head in my hands in total defeat and said out loud, "There *has* to be a better way!"

Just like with Larry, I picked myself up, dusted myself off, and started to analyze what was happening. Here's what I learned:

- I calculated spending about 15-20 hours per week on my foundational content marketing.

- I needed to spend that time focusing on keeping my team and clients happy.
- I was drowning in work, and it wasn't sustainable.
- I was unwilling to become less consistent in my content marketing routine because I knew that consistency was king in online marketing.

That was the moment when the first iteration of the operating procedure for **Leverage To Scale (LTS)** was born.

Here's what I did to get and stay in Alignment with my marketing:

I thought:

- What if I made a quick 5-minute tip video (such as, "The 7 Deadliest Mistakes You're Making In Your Social Media"), then gave that raw video to my CMA (Creative Marketing Assistant) with instructions so they would do keyword research, optimize, and publish the video on YouTube. Then…
- Ask my CMA to craft a compelling blog post (using my words from the video) inviting people to watch the video and spend more minutes with me—which would increase sales conversion. (The blog post would be SEO optimized, of course). Then…
- Ask my CMA to do all of my daily social media for me, plus…
- Send that blog post out as our newsletter to my email community each week. (By driving subscribers back to my website to view the video post, we naturally generated more sales.) And finally…
- Track the growth metrics from all channels and send me a report each Friday.

And further, what if I could offload more than one video each week to my team? What would it take to give me a break from marketing for a while??

Later that week, on Saturday afternoon, I grabbed a latte and sat in my office for the next three hours. In five minutes I created a content plan that offered me a year's worth of video topics (see the training video in your Toolkit for instructions). I then proceeded to bang out almost 25 tip videos. The lift was heaviest in the beginning, but after that first video was complete, flow state kicked in and the rest unfolded quickly. I was on fire!

I gave my team the videos with instructions on how to do the rest of my content marketing and then didn't have to think about ANY of it for the next 25 WEEKS until I needed to give them more video content.

As I shared at the start of this book journey, I embedded the *Leverage To Scale* foundational marketing operation into my platform, and the results still astound me to this day:

→ **After less than one year of implementing the operation consistently** (my part took seven total hours inside two recording sessions), **I had to stop.** Yep, I didn't produce much new content because we had too many qualified leads coming in. #PositiveProblem.
- (Remember, The Work reveals our unique motivators in growth, and not everyone wants to scale in the way you might. I've always wanted a more manageable business.)
- I have since published bursts of content to keep lead flow steady and to generate the amount of speaking opportunities I want, but I never had to wonder where my next client was coming from. The operation has worked better than I could have imagined, and this program now supports brands around the world in the same way.

→ **I cut my personal time spent on marketing activities by 90%.**
- Whereas I originally averaged 15 hours per week on marketing (780 hours annually), the LTS approach took less than 10 hours of my time in that calendar year, and I was able to delegate the rest of the work successfully.
- I was freed up to spend intentional time every day dedicated exclusively to the practice of spreading my cause via speaking (instead of the busywork my team was better suited for). This is non-negotiable because I know it will give me the Impact and reward I want to experience in life.

→ **The company was far better protected.**
- When you hire an outside marketing agency and they fall short, you are forced to start all over with someone new. My strategy kept a well-performing marketing operation in-house, giving us control and peace of mind long-term.

→ **We experienced significant cost savings.**
- Not only did we save tens of thousands of dollars avoiding agency fees by keeping the work in-house, but the operation protected us from team-related sunk costs.
- Most small companies have no training documentation, so when they hire a new person, it requires a significant amount of time and energy to train that individual. With LTS, the training takes a small handful of hours. If a team member exits the organization, a new hire can quickly go through the training and pick up where the last left off in the same week.
- Further, since the operation was repeatable each week, we saved unnecessary costs from the ever-changing chaos that a lot of business owners experience.

→ **Attracted in more qualified buyers.**
  - Because I was only talking to Heather in each of my videos, more Heathers were attracted in. Prospects would watch me for more minutes because the content was video-based. They would form a deeper connection with me by watching more and more videos, then come into a call saying, "Amber! I feel like I already know you…"

→ **Freedom, baby!**
  - I wasn't tied to my office chair each week doing my own marketing. To know a big part of your business is operating well without much input from you is a truly glorious feeling. My pressure decreased while my authority and credibility continued to grow quickly over time.

My platform was in Alignment and operating harmoniously. Growth was inevitable.

And the icing on the cake? This simple operation allowed me to land dozens of strategic partnerships that wanted to refer clients our way because the trust and follow-through factors were so high. More event planners and community leaders asked me to speak, and fees grew higher and higher. It was thrilling! Requests came in to be interviewed on podcasts, and our bottom line grew in ways I couldn't have predicted.

What's more, as I have coached clients through this process, I have seen them experience similar results. When you do The Work and trust yourself to apply it to your sales and marketing, it feels like magic unfolds week in and week out.

For more than ten years I've operated the same marketing strategy, and it continues to bring healthy and satisfying results for both NGNG and our clients!

The only adjustment I recently made was to lean in to personally writing more captions and emails based on the evidence that authenticity drives bigger results. It is a strategy that fosters higher resonance, stronger differentiation, and therefore better conversion. As we've discussed, in today's age, writing must be genuine, full of conviction, emotion-driven, deep, and thoughtful. (If you want to stand out from the computer-generated content that the majority is using, that is.) Writing has become one of the best uses of my time as a business owner, so it stays on my activity list, and I just have to protect my time and energy for it.

When it comes to producing content, I have a well-organized weekly content plan, a clear structure around what I want to say, and total conviction when saying it. You can do the same without it feeling like your marketing efforts are taking up your already limited time.

Here's what it can look like to be in Alignment with your marketing:

- You take care of your well-being so you can show up in a powerful, energetic, magnetic way. You unsubscribe and unfollow others on an as-needed basis to stay empowered. You protect your social feeds and only allow content creators who uplift you and model your Values.
- You give away the farm for free because you practice what you preach: you are doing this for the Impact.
- You create content for your singular Avatar. You get rid of the "masses mentality" and stay focused on what you are here to do: Impact individuals consistently over a long period of time.

- You're unwilling to rely heavily on an AI bot to *create marketing content for you*. (I'm all for using AI as a tool, but not to speak on my behalf.) You prioritize quality, sharing inner wisdom, and making genuine connections with your followers.

- You implement marketing operations that keep your content production consistent because you know your Avatar relies on that to get the help they need. You continue to promote your cause no matter how long it takes to be heard at the scale you desire.

- You know video is the most powerful way to connect with people in a digital world, therefore you put in the effort to lead your marketing practice with this format.

- When you look at photos of yourself, watch yourself on video, or listen to yourself in an interview or on a podcast, you feel confident in what you have to say.

- You recognize you can only make so much happen in a given window of time. Therefore, you value devoting yourself to the practice of marketing each day, trusting you will hit a nerve in the marketplace when it's your turn for the spotlight. You trust your role in the greater harmony of the marketplace, and that the right, qualified customers will continue to be attracted toward you.

Do you see how The Work interacts with your sales and marketing in a very natural way when you are in Alignment?

I successfully grew and operated my company for more than a decade and through the $1,000,000 annual threshold with less than 20 team members (all part-time contractors) by getting in Alignment with my sales and marketing. My foundational operations were congruent and working well.

WHAT ALIGNMENT LOOKS LIKE IN OPERATIONS

You're only as good and strong as your team (quality, communication, workflow), so it makes sense to focus energy on them the best you know how while committing to improve consistently over time.

I try to operate based on the principle "treat others the way you'd want to be treated," and that non-negotiable has worked well for me (especially through the growing pains of my 2020 fast growth). For example:

- I choose to offer healthy compensation and pay my team weekly because if the roles were reversed, I'd want that too.
- I focus on being disciplined as a leader to limit chaos and offer a more empowering work environment.
- As the world has grown more contentious, I enacted rules with my clients and team to limit conflict. In our communication policies, I ask each individual to refrain from sharing political or religious views, to respect personal time outside of normal operating hours, plus offer a list of best practices so we get our best work out of one another (even down to encouraging the use of please and thank you).

I take it upon myself to operate from a high standard and cultivate the environment I want to live in each day. My team values that and therefore protects the culture and wants to see the company succeed long-term.

AmberV's View of Operations: An awareness of why something matters, accompanied by the implementation of a system that supports its execution as efficiently as possible to enhance your team's experience, overall reputation, and personal fulfillment.

Here's what it can look like to be in Alignment with your operations:

- You recognize that your team members are the biggest believers in you and your vision and, therefore, should be treated as such. Be present and delight in little moments with them.
- You include them in conversations around your Foundational Four so that they can help ensure the company stays in Alignment.
- You spend time writing cards, hand-making gifts, and/or participating in experiences with your team so they know without a shadow of a doubt that they are more to you than just an employee stamping out work for you.
- You set your team up for success by investing in training programs that add to their skill set, grow their confidence, and make them more successful in their role.
- You publicly praise your team so your following and strategic partners respect them as much as you do.
- When you get the slightest whiff that a team member is having an off day, you promptly offer a call, offer the day off, and/or offer support.
- You keep your (business) house clean and organized out of respect and appreciation for the opportunity to do your work in the world.
- You embody a high degree of responsibility in follow-through with any and all communication so nothing slips through the cracks. If you need help, delegate or ask for help. The buck stops with you.

- When you get overwhelmed and want to take a beat, you open up a blank piece of paper and dump everything on your mind into that document. Then, share it with your team so they can help you through the messy moment, and together you re-Align and move forward.

WHAT DID WE LEARN?

Throughout my business journey, I operated by a specific set of non-negotiables that not only allowed for the success of my business but also the success of the authors, coaches, and companies we serve.

I learned to attract qualified, engaged buyers who convert into raving customers by:

1. Tweaking the description of my audience, adding a short video to my website home page, and offering a pricing menu PDF with a short opt-in nurture sequence.
2. Batch recording short tip videos twice a year and giving my team training to run my marketing operation.

As a result of sticking with my non-negotiables, NGNG has never been in debt, and we continue to have a deep and wide Impact.

NGNG's story reinforces the value of strategy.

I think of strategy in terms of the fastest way to achieve a goal without sacrificing quality.

We saved an exorbitant amount of time (and therefore saved an exorbitant amount of cash) by implementing Aligned strategies. They were simple and congruent.

In your own business/author journey, there is extreme value in hiring a strategist because you'll save tremendous time, money, energy, and heartache from do-it-yourself guesswork.

We are at a unique time in online business growth where "more is not more" anymore. The pendulum is swinging back in the direction of "less is more."

By activating more strategies, you're only scratching the surface of the potential of each. The invitation is to go deeper and longer with fewer strategies to reap the rewards you sense are possible.

Most entrepreneurs grind and push, force and pull, to achieve their Vision. They experience setbacks and tears, embarrassment, and financial loss. I'm advocating for a more natural way forward.

This chapter has shown you how NGNG Enterprises has navigated sales, marketing, and operations. I've hinted at how those successes within my own business have helped me achieve similar results for those I serve, but this next chapter will take a deeper dive into my approach to developing customized and ALIGNED strategies for entrepreneurs.

By doing The Work, paying attention to the activities that give you more energy, and considering your constraints, we can build a strategy that keeps you in Alignment, generates plenty of revenue, and furthers your Impact.

CHAPTER 11

STRATEGY

"Our plans miscarry because they have no aim. When a person does not know what harbor they are making for, no wind is the right wind."
- Seneca

My brain has been wired to make connections quickly. I can almost instantaneously consider all options, weed out ones that aren't fitting to create maximum leverage and results, and then synthesize that down to an actionable sequence of steps. This wasn't a gift, it was earned.

If I distill my childhood experience, I'd tell you I felt very vulnerable to threats. I was scared and anxious *a lot*. This was a perfect environment to create a busy mind that avoids threats and maximizes wins. A mind that is masterful at strategic planning. When I was young, I'd develop strategies to be myself in a way that created less punishment, manipulation, bullying, and shaming. Now I develop strategies to help awesome humans do more good in the world.

How does strategy fit in with everything you've learned and experienced so far?

- The Work in chapters 5-8 is what gets you into Alignment so you're ready for Impact.
- A strategist like me designs your most leveraged marketing, sales, and operations strategies to achieve your goal as fast as possible without sacrificing quality. (A goal can be launching a #1 bestselling book, getting an extra 3,000 followers, or closing 12 additional sales per month.)
- The strategies are broken down into tasks that your team can be trained on so you collectively achieve that goal.
- All tasks and implemented strategies help you achieve your goals faster, which helps you achieve your Vision of Impact faster.

Hiring the right strategist is of utmost importance. You'll want to have eyes wide open so you select someone who has a deep understanding of your Foundational Four to ensure the strategies are Aligned. It's also incredibly beneficial to collaborate with someone who is trained to help you navigate your resistance so you are ready for the kind of Impact that is in your heart to make.

We don't know what we don't know, right?

- → Everyone seems to be in a rush—but what if your rushed timeline is the wrong strategy for you "right now," and slowing down to speed up is a more Aligned approach? What if slowing down for even a few months meant you could be fully

Aligned, save up to have a bigger budget, allow more time to improve your mental strength for the journey ahead, and have more space to attract a bigger following who would buy more from you?

→ Many people come to me saying they want to build a huge following and have a suite of courses for sale—but what if you're a sensitive introvert who values your calm, quiet lifestyle? Do you think you'll be happy receiving tens of thousands of comments every day, including from trolls who criticize you? What about the inevitable customers who complain about your course and want a refund, or want to waste your time in legal matters? More isn't more anymore.

It's important to note that there is no "right" strategy for everyone. (That's why I can't stand one-size-fits-all approaches to marketing agencies, consulting, and sales growth.)

But there is a "right strategy for YOU."

For example, a business owner who wants to invest $75,000 into their book launch that is 16 months out, who has a 10,000-person audience, with a small team, and can dedicate full-time hours to growing the business would have a completely different strategy than an author who has $7,500 to apply toward a self-published book they want to release in 3 months, with no team, a starting audience of fewer than 500 people, and has a full-time job to work around.

In other leadership books, you'll learn traditional approaches to developing a strategy such as:

1. Define your vision, goals, and objectives.

2. Decide your target "audience" (note: not Avatar).

3. Research current market trends, data, and historicals.

4. Analyze your emerging opportunity and weigh against possible threats.

5. Consider all tactics to employ to reach your objectives.

6. Define your overall strategy.

I don't know about you, but I'm consistently being called forth to innovate a new way of doing business. There is endless room for innovation and improvement.

I personally choose an approach where I research what's traditional, then "go my own way" (...just as the quote on my bathroom wall reminds me to do). I'm interested in speed and maximizing results, which simply requires a more custom approach.

THE AMBERV WAY

[STEP 1]

When someone comes to me for strategic planning, I ask them a series of questions before we even step into a discovery call. I need to understand their **Foundational Four** (a requirement) + **their constraints** so I can start the planning process.

Constraints isn't a negative term here. By looking at the variables, I can very quickly see the fastest way a person can achieve their Vision without sacrificing quality. Constraints can be:

- The size of your team, if any.
- How much time you have each week to dedicate to the amplification of your cause.
- Your budget.
- The quality and size of your existing audience (social media, email lists, network of colleagues, existing clients, etc.).
- Overall timeline to launch or to achieve a certain milestone.
- Your goals (...and everyone's goals are completely different!).
- Industry type and related thought leaders.
- And more...

By distilling this information, I can weed out most options for a client's marketing, sales, and operations strategies.

[STEP 2]

Once I understand your constraints, most of the options presented to you in this very overwhelming online world are eliminated. My job is to protect you and keep you in Alignment! Here's a list of just some of what I'm sifting through:

> MARKETING: Recording video, content writing, podcast interviews, live streams, PR, building complex funnels, hosting webinars, paid advertising, DM outreach, cold outreach emails, deep SEO, and affiliate marketing.
>
> SALES: Books, speaking and events, 1:1 coaching/consulting, courses/programs, membership, masterminds, sponsorship, ad revenue, subscriptions, product e-commerce, affiliate marketing, and being a reseller.
>
> OPERATIONS: Consider team experience, project management, financials, communication, workflow, tech stack, legal, security, training, leadership, customer experience, development, meetings and events, and productivity.

[STEP 3]

After a meaningful and productive discussion, I apply what I've learned into a Business Strategy Map that defines your **marketing, sales, and operations strategies** and offers an Implementation Timeline for your team to manage.

> I've found that most team members need additional training on how to execute an optimized marketing and customer journey plan, so I designed a suite of high-caliber (but low-time commitment and affordable) training programs for you to keep in-house. As you hire new team members, they can simply go through the training and pick up where the previous members left off. (However, when you operate in Alignment, you experience less turnover and more harmony in your operations!)

THIS IS ALL VERY DOABLE FOR YOU.

You've already completed the hard part(!)...
The Foundational Four.

From there, you just want to lock in your goals and strategies, then get the team harmonized to execute with you. And most of that can be done for you!

This truly is the moment you can start to experience momentum (assuming you have an Aligned strategy that protects your energy and time).

Over the years, I've identified a very special, never-widely-discussed approach that holds an invisible space between Step 2 and Step 3 (in the AmberV Way) above.

To experience natural (not forced) success, you must decide on business strategies that maximize *your* natural energy (passion).

A big part of my gift as a strategist is my ability to read people.

I can see when you light up and when you shrink. I use this as a tool to define the "right" strategy for you.

I can feel it when you're hiding and when you are brave. That unspoken data helps guide me to a strategy that unlocks your highest and best *consistently*, so you are better protected and can actually enjoy the road ahead.

I wasn't born with this superpower...I earned it.

I earned it by paying attention (something our society is really struggling with right now).

It started when I was a kid who shrunk when my older sister was in the room. I felt in a constant state of inadequacy around her, since it seemed so natural for her to achieve straight A's, or win Miss Teen Arizona. Meanwhile, it was natural for me to get C's and D's, or fade into the background of any room I was in. I couldn't help but be present to the way my physical body felt heavy and defeated.

I paid attention to what it felt like when my dad took me as a kid into his shop to teach me how to build something with stained glass or fidget with his latest woodworking project. Every minute of one-on-one time meant so much because, per the custody arrangement, I was only able to see him four days a month. Likewise, when my mom was home to tuck me in, and would tell me she could see stars in my eyes, I observed feeling special. I still yearn for that feeling to fill the holes in my heart that surface from time to time.

When my mom forced me to be on stage at a senior care home talent show as a kid, I observed how much I hated being on stage in front of an audience. Yet, when I spoke on stage in front of 300 college students as a 21-year-old, I was invigorated. That contradiction forced me to "pay attention" to the differences between those two experiences to better understand what is happening when I am at my best (feeling empowered) vs. when I'm at my worst (feeling sickened). In this review, I noticed that when I was in the spotlight to be shown off as a cute kid, I felt embarrassed. However, when I was in service, teaching an audience while in the spotlight, I felt connected to something greater than myself, which felt empowering. Exploring these experiences specifically helped inform my business model and part of my marketing strategy.

By peeling back that onion and digging deeper, we can see with great clarity *how we are uniquely designed to serve.*

Why are we addressing feelings so much when we're supposed to be talking about strategy?

1. How we feel impacts how we treat others, which impacts how they feel, which then shifts how we feel. Mutual reciprocation is the mantra to adopt. <u>Therefore, let's make business decisions that keep you feeling your best!</u>

2. With the rise of misinformation, it will get harder and harder for consumers to know what's true. This forces audiences to develop their intuitive muscle and their emotional guidance system. Brands that don't lead with authentic, emotion-based influence will fall behind.

So, I'll say again: <u>To experience natural (not forced) success, you must decide on business strategies that maximize *your* natural energy (passion).</u>

It wasn't long after starting NGNG that I knew it wasn't enough to keep operating solely by my non-negotiables…

I innovated The Work, reviewed my constraints, and observed what elevated my natural energy. In consideration of those three things, my marketing and sales strategies flowed from there.

All I had to do was trust my intuition to know what was right for me.

(And, when you're in doubt of what your intuition is saying, go back to the Foundational Four for clarity to help you make decisions.)

As we progress, and I share my strategies below, be thinking about which strategies appeal to you, which don't, and why, so you can then ideate a list of strategies that maximize your natural energy.

NGNG'S MARKETING STRATEGY

<u>Word of mouth</u>

>This is by far the most powerful form of advertising. By staying focused on my non-negotiables, word of mouth took off. Since

then, I haven't had to wonder where my next client would come from.

Recording video

> Video as a strategy is paramount because the more minutes someone watches you on video, the stronger their trust and desire to work with you grows. I enjoy imagining Heather sitting at her messy desk, sipping coffee, and watching me as a positive outlet in her day. I see her getting inspiration. I'm part soul food to her, and that makes me feel special. It's so important to me to know she's getting value, she's making progress, she's feeling more motivated and powerful, and she's feeling worthy again.

Podcast interviews and live streams

> The obvious strategy is to grow my audience by getting exposure to other people's communities. I look at that as the icing on the cake, though. My primary strategy is to connect with the podcast or livestream host (the community leader). This can lead to far bigger opportunities such as developing friendships, speaking at workshops or events, and getting introduced to others in my peer group; and in many cases, it can lead to the host hiring me for strategy, web design, marketing, and/or book launch support.

What is not presently in our marketing activity list: PR, producing content using AI, building complex funnels, hosting webinars, paid advertising, spamming people with DMs, cold outreach spam emails, deep SEO, and affiliate marketing.

Why? Because I've done The Work to see that these strategies are not in Alignment either because Heather wouldn't engage in those activities, they are not congruent with my Values, or they give me a serious energy drain. I engage in activities that light me up! This is true for the following sections in this chapter as well.

NGNG'S SALES STRATEGY

Publishing books

> As discussed strategically, launching a great book is the fastest way to scale your Impact. It works wonders to grow your following and revenue and to establish your authority, intention, value, and differentiation. It keeps you relevant, opens opportunities for speaking and joint ventures, and offers you discipline, focus, and structure. It can be very cathartic, nurturing, and fulfilling. It documents your legacy and can offer so much to your family for generations to come. Need I continue? (Speaking of…check out my son's book, *The Long Forest Trail*, on Amazon. My hope is that it would inspire your little ones to write a book, or offer you ideas on how to share your cause with a younger audience.)

Speaking and events

> I am very passionate about virtual and in-person facilitation, speaking, teaching, and coaching for small groups. I experience tremendous joy in hosting my own three-day *Books & Business* in-person events. I commit to occasional big-stage in-person speeches at large conferences.

> Speaking and events are key strategies to get your cause out to the world more quickly, just like with podcast interviews. However, my strategy within these three areas of speaking and events listed above is to make individual connections with each person in the room (virtual or in-person).

Key Note: Notice how my Vision interacts with this strategy…For example, when speaking in front of 500 photographers at the national PPA conference, I stood by the door welcoming each guest before we began. I cruised up and down the aisles shaking hands, offering big smiles, and asking the audience what would make this speech the best use of their time. I leaned in, gave hugs, and shared advice, connecting with as many people as possible before ever walking on stage. During the speech, I made intentional eye contact, flashed smiles, and referenced names and needs. Afterward, time was spent with each person in line who waited to share words of thanks with me. I offered more smiles, enjoyed more hugs, received their gratitude, and continued to give. I gave every ounce of myself to that group. My Vision and Why were fulfilled. I was in Alignment, making a far bigger Impact than just on the 500 individuals in attendance. They will carry forward the feeling, the Impact, the teaching, and the gestures so that others can experience it too.

A small invite-only mastermind

This is a special, private offer to attendees of my Books & Business event for deep conversation on business and life each month. This is a strategy to keep me intellectually and spiritually engaged in my work. Every business owner needs an outlet with peers to open up and share their real thoughts and feelings to get encouragement and support. I wanted to offer a safe space for the people I love and respect (my community) because my Core Value is better together. See how The Work informs the strategy again?

1:1 strategic planning

I loooove one-on-one calls with change-makers more than anything else I do in the entire business. I have no awareness of the hours that pass, and I almost never experience an energy drain (even though I'm introvert-leaning, which surprises a lot of people!). If my incredible COO didn't build breaks and stops into my schedule, I'd be on calls for 12 hours a day, no problem.

Key Note: It makes more strategic sense to "scale profit" using just about any other type of offering—courses, stage speaking, annual corporate programs, etc. Trading dollars for hours doesn't make sense to a lot of people. However, scaling profit wasn't in my Vision statement, was it? My Vision is to help others feel seen, heard, and valued. And, my Why is to receive that very thing. So, it makes perfect sense that I would thrive in a 1:1 environment because that is when I experience congruence, my highest possible value output, and, in return, deep personal fulfillment.

- *THIS is why we must take the time and persevere through doing The Work. It completely informs our "right" unique business strategies that leave us feeling free, energized, and ready for more.*

- To be clear, you can absolutely make a great living by focusing on what you love.

I now only take on ten "all-in" strategic planning clients at a time. This was a strategy to offer my best work to the most serious clients who most wanted to work with me. I have room in my schedule to offer on-demand strategy sessions and coaching to individuals who need help here and there. Everyone else who wants to engage with me but can't due to these schedule constraints can get extremely high value out of my NGNG Academy and Books & Business Membership.

The NGNG Academy

This is where we house a suite of hyper-specific, deep-dive training programs to teach *your team* how to execute strategy with and for you. My best work, templates, spreadsheets, SOPs, and examples are all housed inside these programs so they are widely accessible.

Books & Business Membership

This is a month-to-month membership for committed, impact-driven entrepreneurs. It's a place I can pour into each individual to ensure they are focused, Aligned, and getting fresh strategies to move forward within all areas of their business. I openly give the community assets as I build them, and share my personal best practices for growth. One of the things I've always received the most praise for is the caliber of my network, and inside this membership, people are forging life-long collaborative relationships. It's a very special environment!

What is not presently in our sales activity list: sponsorship, ad revenue, subscriptions, product e-commerce, affiliate marketing, being a reseller, etc. Remember, I follow activities that light me up, and we've achieved a high-Impact seven-figure business out of that core belief.

WHICH STRATEGY IS RIGHT FOR YOU?

The strategies above are a taste of what's possible. They are not here to stir up comparison, only to offer new perspectives and **guide you toward what is right for YOU**.

→ If a strategy makes you feel drained, unhappy, brain-foggy, or stressed, consider if you want to KEEP the strategy but delegate it to a team member, or if you want to eliminate the strategy from your business model.

→ If a strategy makes you feel enthusiastic while offering a positive challenge and smiles, keep it.

→ If a strategy brings up fear, resistance, or insecurity, I recommend you try it twice before you decide if you keep or eliminate it from your model. You want to be certain the strategy is the issue, and not your resistance flaring up.

→ Try very hard NOT to make decisions based on what you think will drive the most revenue. Instead, pay attention to your emotions and physicality so we ensure all strategies are in Alignment with what lights you up (otherwise, other issues will crop up in the business).

Strategic planning will be an evolving need for you.

That's why some clients work with me for many years or haven't stopped at all. As technology advances and trends change, your model will need to adapt, and your strategies will adjust. Additionally, you are evolving as a human, so therefore your cause is evolving, and that will also require change over time. And that is ok. Having a trusted advisor by your side to help you navigate these moments is a powerful asset for any business owner.

==Nature teaches us that change is inevitable. Therefore, we have an invitation to revisit our definition of change and not be so afraid or set back by it.==

Please know that I am not always in perfect practice with my strategies or my company at large. Running a business has kicked my ass on lots of occasions.

I've made wrong hires and shotgun decisions that cost me a lot in the end, collaborated with people I now wish I wouldn't have, and so much more. I will continue to share openly with you so you have a resource who is brave enough to take you behind the curtain. That's what my Books & Business membership community was designed for. *(You get open, honest communication with me. You can get smoke and mirrors elsewhere.)*

We are all human. We all make mistakes, but we hopefully learn from them (eventually) and improve.

Be patient with your progress. Continue to focus on giving, adapting, and growing.

Surround yourself with people who want to see you succeed. Allow them to pour into you so you stay open and experience Infinite Impact with your cause. I'd love to continue to stand by your side as a fellow traveler beyond this book.

You now have the tools and resources to
get and stay in Alignment, and apply The Work
to your Books & Business.
That is HUGE!!

Before you flip to the final chapter, I invite you to
reset the space around you and get cozy before I
offer you a vulnerable share.

Sending so much gratitude your way...

xo,
Amber V

Email me at amber@infiniteimpactbook.com
with the subject line:
"I'M NOW READY TO MAKE INFINITE IMPACT"
for a big congratulations.

PART FOUR

SCALE YOUR IMPACT

CHAPTER 12

INFINITE IMPACT

*"Do the thing you fear
and the death of fear becomes certain."
- Fortune Cookie*

If you had spent any amount of time with me in the early 2020s or prior, it wouldn't have taken you long to notice I apologized for everything. (Especially things I had no involvement with.) If we arrived at a restaurant on time for our reservation and there was a five-minute wait, I'd apologize. If we grabbed a coffee and yours was too hot or too cold, I'd apologize. It was so natural and automatic that I didn't even notice it except when people would look at me strangely and tell me that I didn't need to apologize. I never worked too hard to change that habit, figuring there were a lot worse personality traits than over-apologizing. (And I certainly hadn't realized how much this pointed to my people-pleasing behavior, *let alone question where that stemmed from*.)

Well into adulthood, I hadn't felt a need to analyze my childhood experiences too closely. I was perfectly fine clinging to my rose-colored glasses. I wasn't denying what happened—I just chose to focus on the good times, while finding a logical reason to justify the ugly times. In general, I thought things were pretty buttoned up.

I worked harder and harder to uphold an insane personal standard in all areas of my life in hopes of attracting more good experiences and repelling the bad as much as humanly possible. If I were loving, honest, well-groomed, positive-minded, a neat freak, well-organized, fast at getting things done, smart, independent, funny, and accomplished... then I'd make friends and the bullies would go away.

As ugly things continued to happen (almost as if orchestrated), I became more resilient at picking myself up, dusting myself off, filing the experience away, and continuing to march down "the light path" to make the world a better place.

<u>To boil it down, I pushed myself to the extreme to get more love, but if I got dumped on, I'd justify it out of avoidance and keep moving forward.</u> That high-standard, rose-colored mindset was effective until I neared my 40th birthday.

Whereas I was once proud of my strength and self-proclaimed level-headedness, the sheer fight to stay positive (<u>while ignoring certain truths</u>) was exhausting. I calculated what it would take to maintain this warrior's pace, and the results were grim.

I knew I had to find a more natural—not forced—way to experience life.

What I craved the most was a feeling of freedom—*naturally free to be the real me* **and** *be loved as a result.*

Authentic & Loved.

If I didn't have to push so hard to be perfect to avoid bad things happening, maybe I could use that saved energy to *enjoy* my life. (I knew deep down this was the way forward.)

<u>This meant I had to disarm the invisible protection I'd made from memories and beliefs that scared me.</u>

That armor was built after I was jumped when I was 16, and every difficult memory prior was sewn into the fabric. It helped me graduate with honors, break national records with Cutco, start a family, grow my company, and help so many impact-makers around the world. *Who would I be if I let my walls down?! And yet, where would my exhaustion lead me if I didn't try...?*

In the following two to three years, I experienced the deepest, hardest, scariest work of my life to uncover *why* I did the things I did. It was an incredibly mind-blowing blessing.

Any author who writes a book that's meaningful to them will tell you that all of your messiness comes up in the process of writing. (Boy, was that true for me writing this book.) I've grieved deeply and celebrated quite fully in the course of writing these pages for you. You are experiencing all of me and all I've been through, not just in story or teaching topic, but in each word that was carefully chosen with a life's worth of experiences parked beneath them.

Publishing can be very scary because we know there are people in the world who won't be conscious in their response, and we're afraid of being changed by their negativity. That resistance fires off storm sirens begging us not to publish anything too personal, fighting for our protection.

My greatest fear around publishing something so intimate was that I would be misunderstood, it wouldn't be well-received, and I feared that I would follow the all-too-familiar pattern of hiding afterward. I feared I would collect the wrong evidence and that it would ultimately keep me small.

My people-pleasing mentality was flaring up again.

In my final days of writing, I examined why that fear was coming up, and most importantly, where it stemmed from.

In moments like this, I remember my NGNG mantra and the fortune cookie I got years ago that reminds me to lean into my fears so I am no longer afraid.

I traced that feeling of fear in a guided session with my mentor Dimitri. I landed in a scene that I don't have an official memory of, yet it felt *incredibly* real. Maybe it happened and I suppressed it, or maybe it was my imagination offering a summation of what my childhood felt like.

> *I was three years old, sitting alone in a large foyer that branched off into three different rooms. The shiny saltillo tile was cool on my chubby little legs. I sat on the floor in a dress with curled cloth on the ends. I was happy. The house felt safe to me. This was before my parent's divorce two years later, before my mom was away so much, before my older sister grew angry for having to take care of me, before knowing there was such a thing as not being well-liked in school or getting punished for any number of things I'd done wrong, or other volumes of stories that hurt to think about.*

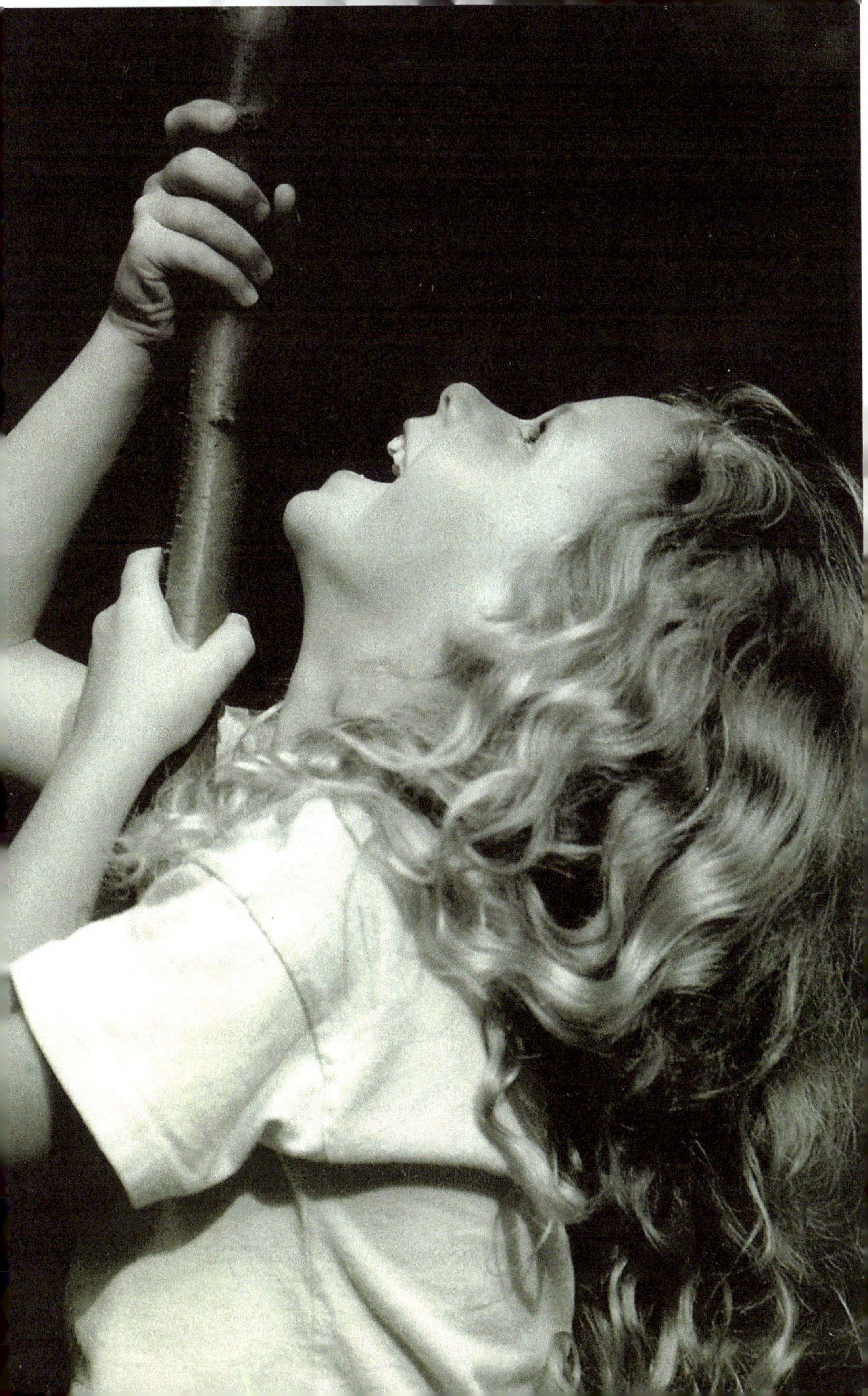

In this scene, I was at peace. I saw my sister's teddy bear in front of me. It was a big, brown, frumpy bear that was almost as tall as I was at that age. His face and belly had been worn down from the constant love my sister gave him. He was her absolute favorite.

Just then, my sister stomped toward me. Her jelly sandals made a loud smacking sound on the floor. She screamed at me to give her Teddy back. I offered a slow response of surprise and confusion. I honestly wasn't sure what was happening. I hadn't taken her stuffy, I was just playing with what was in front of me. She stormed off, yelling down the hallway for Mom.

I continued to play by matching the size of my hand with how big Teddy's paw was. I smiled and giggled a little in delight. He was so big and cuddly.

The next thing I knew, my sister was dragging my mom closer to me. She was crying again and complaining to my mom about how unfair it was. I couldn't understand half of what she was saying, but I knew I didn't want her to be upset. I cared for her. Did she want to play with Teddy and me together? That would be so fun!

Mom looked down on me and told me to give the bear back. She sighed, and I could tell she was upset for some reason too. I was trying to understand what I had done wrong. My sister ripped the bear out of my loose hand-hold. Mom turned and walked away with my sister following her and saying words I couldn't hear.

The only thing I'd understood was that somehow it was my fault.

The session with Dimitri carried deep and profound meaning for my life.

Again, I don't know if that experience actually unfolded or if it was a nod to the many, many times a similar dynamic played out between the three of us. And it doesn't matter because it's less about what happened and more about the meaning I assigned to it. What does matter is that I unknowingly clung to a set of beliefs that shaped my life—believing I was second best to my sister, that I was unsafe being happy, that things were always my fault (sorry!), and more.

Most pertinently, I could quickly trace this root experience forward, through decades of my life where relationship encounters reinforced my belief that I would be misunderstood and pay a price for it.

(No wonder I was feeling afraid to publish my life's learning in a book.)

A full-circle moment I celebrated was now being able to fall back on a framework that could help me further build my own Courage to Course-Correct. In my final days of writing, I went back to Chapter 3, and I did the exercise again.

Instead of reinforcing the belief that I'd be misunderstood…I reinforced the belief that when I show up fully self-expressed, with a passion to help others feel seen, heard, and valued…I too would be seen, heard, and valued.

By staying in Alignment, we experience mutual reciprocation between our Vision and Why, our life's purpose is actualized, and we are left feeling deeply fulfilled.

This is a more natural—not forced—way to get our cause out into the world. This process helps us re-focus on what we can *give*.

I share so openly and honestly with you because you will have similar experiences moving forward on your journey. You may experience hesitation, fear, discomfort—insert your word choice—as you go to launch or share your cause. You may be living with buried self-doubt, anxiety, or loneliness. Someone wronged us, and we wronged someone else. It all stems from a deep wound.

My mom always said, "The grass grows, the wind blows, and people do what they do."

We are humans evolving. That's why unconsciously judging, shaming others, and fueling contention has to stop. We all come from a past that includes heartache, grief, rejection, and a lack of self-love. By addressing what we may have misinterpreted, we can shift our perspective as adults, heal from all that did *and didn't* happen, and powerfully move forward to craft a deeply fulfilling legacy.

<u>However, this kind of legacy requires the courage to drop the protective armor, stay open, and choose to be fully self-expressed.</u>

And don't you secretly crave that anyway?

What if life didn't have to feel so compartmentalized?

At the end of the day, this is the question that guides my life:

Who would you be proud to be?

When I ask that question, I let answers come from my soul, not my approval-seeking mind.

I personally want to know I put it all on the line and lived my life to the max. I want to steadily move through my fears and trust the calling in my heart to serve. I want to stay in Alignment and show (not just tell) my son what it means to have self-trust, self-love, and ultimately be fully self-expressed. That's who I would be proud to be.

We must fight our natural instincts to hide parts of ourselves away, for only when we remain open can we truly connect with others and create positive influence more naturally.

It takes a LOT of guts to lean into your fear, insecurity, resistance, and ignorance and take action to help others, especially after you've been hurt badly in the past.

We are not victims, though.

This is an invitation to take back the power you gave away to those you were hurt by.

The truth is, the pain we endured was a catalyst for the cause we are now called to share with others. And what a gift that is…

I'm not letting anyone off the hook, and I am a new, happy student of boundary-setting.

With awareness comes better choices. It's an eyes-wide-open approach to choosing who we surround ourselves with…and I want to surround myself with people who are responsible in their care of me. I can choose to welcome people into my life who want me to open up, who appreciate my efforts, and who understand my purpose, while excusing those who don't reciprocate and instead manipulate or shame me.

When we take back our power, it lightens the load of our burdens.

With a lighter load, our vocal cords open up and are free to express more naturally. (And let's be honest, your own silence has caused more than enough disconnection and isolation. No more…)

And now, with the ability to use our voice, we can speak louder than the voices of rejection. We can speak louder than the noise of generic, surface content.

The invitation is to do The Work to make your backpack lighter for the road ahead, and instead, fill it full of supplies that are life-giving and not life-taking.

I honor the necessity for both of us to engage in The Work and support one another as we pursue Infinite Impact together.

xo,

Amber V

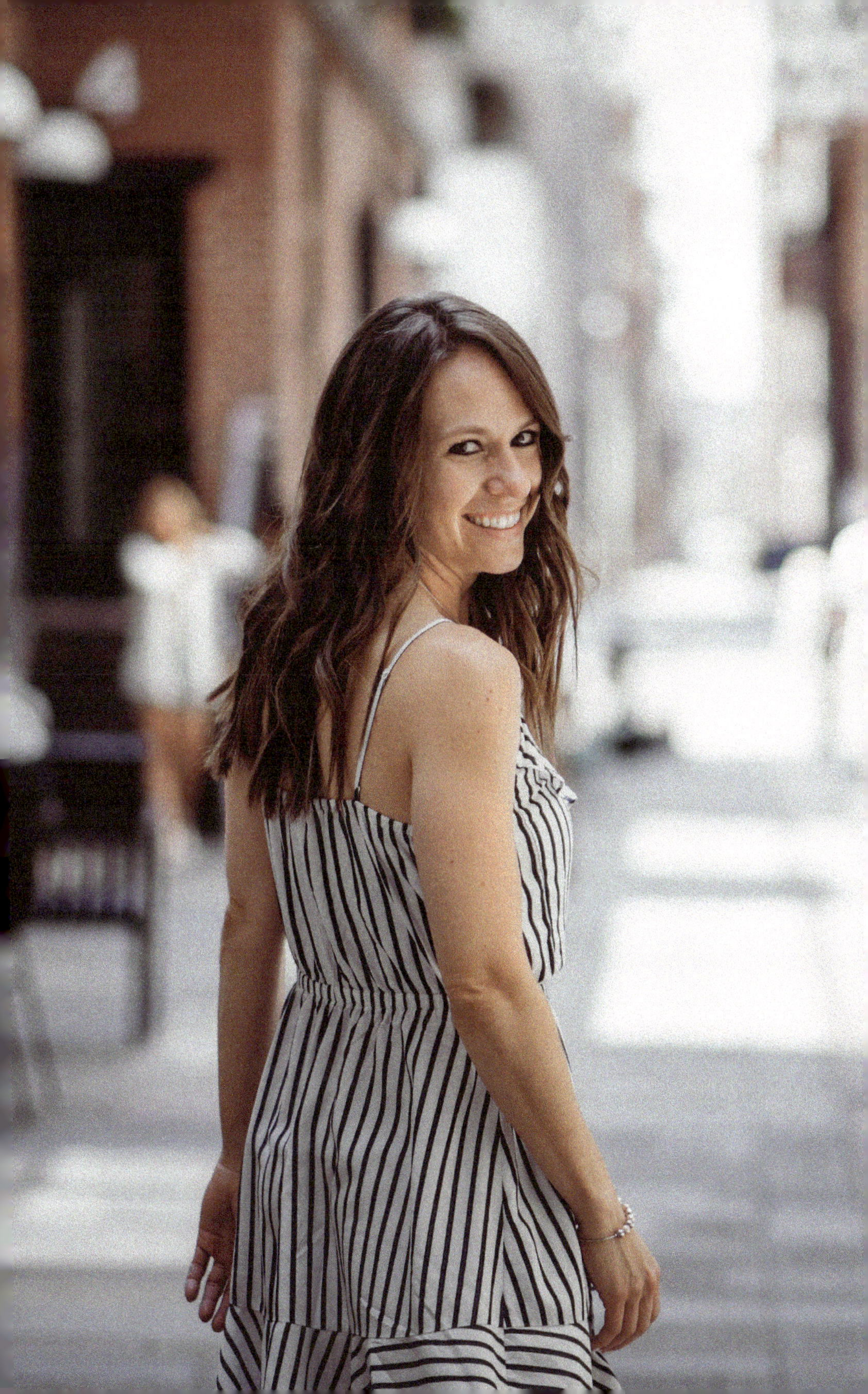

ACKNOWLEDGMENTS

This book may have poured out of me in less than three months, but the wisdom inside was a lifetime in the making. Forty years of growth, heartbreak, accomplishment, setbacks, friendships coming and going, smiles, tears, phone calls, post-it notes, concerts, brush strokes, travel, and coffee shop visits.

I genuinely thank every person I've ever met, and sit in gratitude for every "I love you" and every rejection I ever received.

I imagine myself as a little girl…alone in her bedroom playing with her My Little Pony… looking up at me now. She had no idea what was in store for her, but she dreamed that someday she would have others to play with.

And now, **dear reader**, you are the newest member of this incredible community of entrepreneurs who aren't afraid to do the work and rise and shine every morning to meet the day with impact-driven determination. **Thank you** for your trust, time, and encouragement.

This book would not have seen the light of day without the light of my life…**my son, Clay**. For decades I focused on making decisions based on the question, "Who would I be proud to be?" The bar has been raised significantly since this little one came into my life. From the moment he and I first touched cheek-to-cheek, it has been an honor to support his greatness. Knowing him has given me more courage than I ever knew possible to slay my dragons. I have unlimited energy to advocate for the protection of his—and all other kid's—future. *(That's why I urge you to take massive action with this book and help make our world a better place!)*

A deep and profound thank you…

To my **dad**. "If I had a flower for every time I thought of you, I could walk through my garden forever." - Alfred Lord Tennyson. I once danced with my dad. He gripped me so tightly. He leaned in and whispered, "I wish I could know you forever." Words can't express my gratitude for his love, consistency, groundedness, and wisdom that has helped me rise again after many brutal moments in the valley.

To my **mom**. "Dare to be different." No one has had a more profound impact on my life. She was present in every line of this book, and her wisdom will be felt for generations to come. (I'll see you "somewhere out there," mom.)

To my life-reviving consciousness coach, **Dimitri Therios**. When two years ago it felt like a nuclear bomb went off in my belief system after a major life event, this man worked tirelessly to help me rebuild, get aligned, and thrive once more. His dedication, total acceptance, and unwavering love are unlike anything I've ever experienced. Truly, one in more than eight billion.

*To my seriously incredible, loving, committed, **all-star team**.*

Some team members supported me for a season, and my respect and gratitude for their time and dedication will continue to flow for the rest of my life because they influenced our important work in the world.

Then, there are those who connected with me on a deeper and more meaningful level, and who continue to serve our collective vision, bringing their best to the table day in and day out with no end in sight. Thank you tremendously for choosing me!

Some have created an unbreakable core that has Impacted me to levels I find hard to articulate. The respect, friendship, honesty, love, laughs, GREAT work, passion, and play…All I can say is that wherever you are, is where I want to be…An extra special thank you to **Alexis Snell** who endured long days and late nights, pouring herself into this process to make sure the essence of our work was properly captured, these pages were beautiful, and I found the courage to release them to the world. **Megan O'Malley** for her unwavering positive vibes and invaluable leadership in creating meaningful connection with our community. Megan breathes belief into each of us, making us better every day. **Cierra Warner** for unwavering, spot-on leadership and being a friend to the end. Few have taken the time and care to see me and support me in the way this incredible woman has. She truly makes our world spin round and round. **Lauren Meers** for the depths of her care and dedication—not just in keeping our day-to-day moving forward, and our brand in alignment, but for her personal care to recognize my efforts and fill up my cup at the end of long days.

To **my world-class inner circle** who had a direct impact on the creation and publishing of this book.

> To **Isaac Stegman** for his extreme dedication and acts of service—from holding space through the tears of doubt to challenging word choices (encouraging only the very best to come out of me), and for protecting my voice. You've supported me by not only carrying the utmost belief in this book but also in helping shape our core values, encouraging my company's growth, and insightfully offering strategic support along the way.
>
> To **Ashley de Tello** for her above-and-beyond efforts (an understatement) in getting this book edited to be what so many professionals in our industry hoped it would be. Her early belief, the decision to block all other clients out to offer full focus during such a demanding turnaround, and her genuine loving support are things I'll be eternally thankful for.
>
> To **Ashley Bunting** and her entire team of rockstars for their out-of-this-world attitude, belief, and speed. For *sure* this book wouldn't have hit the market when it did without each of you operating in a brilliant symphony of publishing production. My very deepest gratitude to each of you!
>
> To **Amy Post**. A woman I highly respect for how fiercely she shows up in advocacy for those she loves. Amy is the literal reason why this book came out as quickly as it did. Early on in writing, when I found my own words confrontational and chock-full of accountability, I wanted to slow down my timeline. I wasn't convinced I was ready to be seen and heard to this degree. Amy unknowingly sent a single text message that I took as a sign that

the book needed to come out, and fast. Amy continues to teach me a lot about friendship, just by being her natural self.

To **Kelly Notaras** for entering my life at the perfect moment, and for holding me accountable in the way she did so I would finally get a book out into the world. I cannot wait to live more life together!!

To **Darryll Stinson** for listening to his intuition and doing his own work to get and stay in alignment because, without that, I wouldn't have received the powerful conversation and accountability that is directly responsible for my innovation of the Courage to Course-Correct exercise. Your congruence shaped me, and now, your Impact will be felt infinitely.

To **Sandra Beck** for playing such an important role in this process. Without you, I wouldn't have cleared my schedule to write this book myself. And, without you, the title wouldn't be Infinite Impact (love!).

To my mastermind group, beta readers, book cover voters, and encouraging fans who dropped emails, DMs, and text messages along the way… You have no idea how much each of you offered me oxygen to keep going. It really took a village, and I'm so, so thankful we are connected!

Writing a book is a soulful act. It took real guts for me to be fully self-expressed, and I'm so thankful to cement my life's learnings in this way.

Thank you, dear reader, for the care you expressed by reading these pages. Thank you for using your voice to excitedly share this book with anyone you think could benefit from getting in alignment. Thank you for jumping in with both feet into the Books & Business community.

We welcome you with open arms and are excited to stand strong as a united front to make the world a better place for generations to come.

As a final note, please remember...

It is time to get your cause out to the world in a much faster and more significant way. It is time to dig in and be the leader you know deep down you are meant to be. It is time to eliminate distractions, cultivate the right team to support you, and leverage your talent to scale your impact.

When fear, doubt, or frustration creep in, remember your vision. Remember why you started your business. Remember all of the people out there who are ready to grow their life's meaning, being transformed by the cause you stand for.

Remember, No Guts No Glory!

BOOKS & BUSINESS MEMBERSHIP

Join Our Exclusive Education-Rich Community for Targeted Strategic Advice and Meaningful Connection with Aligned, Impact-Driven Entrepreneurs!

Immerse yourself in a supportive environment where you will learn to further apply the revolutionary principles from the book, network with other like-minded leaders, and fast-track your vision toward a more healthy, profitable, and fulfilling business.

Within this collective, you'll harness the power of courage, alignment, and collaboration to not only elevate your own success but also make a lasting difference in the lives of others. Dive deep into the Foundational Four Framework—Avatar, Vision, Why, and Values—and embark on a journey to unleash your full potential.

With exclusive access to expert guidance, peer support, and actionable strategies, you're not just joining a coaching or mentoring group; you're stepping into a realm of endless possibilities where together we can create an Infinite Impact.

> "Amber has been instrumental in so many ways for my business and for me personally. I've had nothing but impeccable, high-level conversations with her."
>
> — Justin Donald, Lifestyle Investor

> "Amber is the very best at what she does! Everyone knows she is a force of nature but what really differentiates her is her level of care."
>
> — Mark B. Murphy, Northeast Private Client Group

Join the membership today at BooksAndBusiness.com/Members

BOOKS & BUSINESS EVENTS

Learn from the Best in the Industry How Your Business Can Make a Powerful Impact — and a Meaningful Profit — in a Way That Aligns with, and Fulfills You

This annual event is a fan favorite! Each 3-day event features a new curriculum, accompanied by deep workshops and experiences sure to leave you feeling connected and supercharged, ready for Infinite Impact!

- If you want to be surrounded by other driven leaders who care about balance and connectivity…
- If you want incredibly practical knowledge and tools you can use immediately in your business…
- If you're looking for a new perspective, fresh content, and a more leveraged way forward…
- If you're feeling lost when navigating the complexities of the recent major changes in marketing, sales, or achieving impact at scale…

This opportunity will change the trajectory of your life. Books & Business is 85% Business…15% Books…and 100% Fun!

"Hands down one of the best events I've attended in the last 10 years, just based on the level of community and collaboration alone."

— **Rodric Lenhart**

"The generosity and brilliance of the people in this room paid off 10x."

— **Nell Derick Debevoise**

RSVP for our next event at BooksAndBusiness.com/Join

NGNG ACADEMY

Get Your Team the Training They Need to Operate Advanced Marketing and Sales Strategy for Your Books & Business!

A training platform designed to teach your team how to execute the marketing and launch operations as well as strategies discussed in this book. Bestselling programs include:

Leverage To Scale: Train your team to get ALL of your weekly video, social media, blogging, and email marketing done for you. We train your assistant to think and act like an advanced internet marketer to maximize your brand exposure, generate a consistent flow of qualified leads, and condition your audience to buy.

Bestseller Book Launch Blueprint: Learn the day-to-day operations necessary to get bestselling book results in a highly competitive world. We pull back the curtain and share the very conversion strategies used during our most successful book launches including viral live streaming, monetization in advance of the launch, hitting #1, and scaling up.

Relationship Management Operation: The biggest sales impact you can make when launching your book starts by reviving and nourishing current relationships within your existing network. By focusing on cultivating those relationships, you can tap into audiences that wouldn't normally be within your reach. This program offers hours of video training, dozens of email and video examples, spreadsheets, a comprehensive SOP, and more.

> "Thank you so much for putting together this training program. It has taken so much pressure off of me as the business owner and we've seen tremendous results—more than I can really hope for. Most importantly, it's given me headspace so that I can focus on the strategy of the business as we have an amazing system now running in the background."
>
> — Dr. Garric Vosloo

Explore our bestselling programs and get your team trained at NGNGenterprises.com/Programs

STRATEGIC PLANNING

Giving You Strategy, Systems, and Speed to Scale Your Online Business

Having a stellar platform and marketing operation is a HUGE improvement for most business owners, but if you don't have a profitable monetization model, as well as a plan for effectively scaling your business, you won't realize your company's full potential. Hiring the right strategist is of utmost importance—your annual business success and longevity hinges on it. To experience natural (not forced) growth, you need business strategies that maximize your natural energy (passion). Amber Vilhauer focuses on revolutionizing the way her clients scale their business in a way that is profitable, builds a lasting connection with customers, and leaves the business owner feeling deeply fulfilled. All of her strategies are customized to meet your needs and align with your Foundational Four (no generic, cookie-cutter ideas here). The relationship she cultivates with her clients is personal and long-term.

She starts by designing your most leveraged marketing, sales, and operations strategies to achieve your goals as fast as possible without sacrificing quality. Next, Amber breaks the strategies down into tasks that your team can be trained on to reduce your time commitment and pressure. It's this win-win-win approach that keeps clients coming back for more!

"Amber's company NGNG Enterprises is an amazing company to work with—best I've seen in the industry!"
— Pete Vargas, Advance Your Reach

"If you are serious about having a significant launch of your book, product, or personal brand, there is only one source I recommend: Amber Vilhauer. She's extraordinary."
— Mike Michalowicz, bestselling author of *Profit First*

"Hiring Amber was an absolute game-changer! A fantastic experience from beginning to end."
— John Lee Dumas, Entrepreneurs On Fire

Apply for a strategic planning session with AmberV at NGNGenterprises.com/Scale

SPEAKING

Creative and Innovative Solutions to Scale Your Impact-Driven Business

Amber Vilhauer has spoken on international stages, both big and small, for more than a decade. She fully understands the mechanics necessary to engage an audience and empower them for an extraordinary end result.

Event hosts experience a great degree of ease and confidence since Amber understands what is required to put on a wildly successful event.

She pours value into an audience before, during, and after speaking, whether for a 15-minute talk, full-day workshop, or 3-day intensive training seminar.

Her confidence, enthusiasm, potent tactical content, and powerful authenticity create a lasting impression on audiences, regardless of size.

Speaking topics include:

- The most effective strategy to achieve alignment and create Infinite Impact
- How to repeatedly attract and convert qualified buyers
- Elevate every experience and win the attention game online
- Launch and leverage your book for long-term sales success

"I don't promote speakers willy-nilly, but Amber Vilhauer walks the walk."

— Li Hayes, talent and speaker manager

To inquire about fees and availability, please go to AmberVilhauer.com/Speaking

THE LONG FOREST TRAIL

Inviting Parents and Kids to Experience the Power of Connection with Nature and Each Other for Stronger Health and Happiness

The Long Forest Trail is a captivating early reader's children's book, imagined by 6-year-old bestselling author Clay Vilhauer.

Join Clay and his mom on an enchanting journey through nature as they explore a vibrant trail of discovery. Hand in hand, they embark on a colorful adventure through all four seasons, where Clay learns about happiness and resilience while facing challenges from the elements. Through heartfelt conversations, Clay realizes the power of love, trust, kindness, and staying strong through life's obstacles.

The Long Forest Trail is a heartwarming tale celebrating family bonds, resilience, gratitude for nature's wonders, and—above all—the power of human connection.

"Packed with deeper meanings and great discussion points…this book is magical."
— Chip Conley, *New York Times* Bestselling Author and Hospitality Entrepreneur

Thank you for supporting Clay! Get your copy and *please leave a review for him on Amazon.* **Details can be found at: www.ClayVilhauer.com.**

(Please consider placing a substantial bulk order that we can then distribute to foster homes, schools, and children's hospitals. Our goal is to personally distribute 10,000 copies to kids who could really use the gift of empowerment, connection, and self-love!)

ABOUT THE AUTHOR

Amber Vilhauer is the visionary CEO and Founder of NGNG Enterprises (No Guts No Glory), a top strategic planning and marketing agency, and Inc. 5000 award-winner.

In the nearly 20 years she's been building healthy, profitable, impact-driven online brands, Amber has mastered exactly how to design customized and highly leveraged operations to help authors, speakers, and coaches make a sustainable impact that cements their legacy.

As an award-winning leader, Amber has successfully orchestrated countless book launch campaigns, making more than 1,000 authors #1 bestsellers including Les Brown, Lisa Nichols, and Mark Victor Hansen. Her emphasis on personally meaningful and human connection-based outcomes is what sets her apart from traditional internet marketers, contributing to the demand for her as an industry-leading speaker, consultant, and trainer.

Through her compelling story of overcoming adversity and a passion for empowering entrepreneurs, Amber has become a guiding light for authors, speakers, and coaches worldwide.

She currently resides in Northern Colorado with her little boy, who is the #1 joy in her life. They frequent their cabin in the woods to soak in nature, play, and experience adventure on the long forest trails.

Learn more at AmberVilhauer.com

Printed in the USA
CPSIA information can be obtained
at www.ICGtesting.com
LVHW052106020524
778884LV00002B/40